Where on Earth is Heaven?

Arthur E. Travis

Macon, Georgia
1996

ISBN   0-86554-526-X   P141

Where on Earth is Heaven?
Copyright 1996 Arthur E. Travis

Printed in the United States of America.

Previously published
by Broadman Press, Nashville, Tennessee
© 1974 Broadman Press
ISBN 0-8054-1928-4
Library of Congress Catalog Card Number 74-78967

All Scripture citations are from the
American Standard Version unless otherwise indicated.

**The publication of this book has been made possible
through the generosity of Deen Day Smith,
to whom the author and publisher
express their appreciation.**

Contents

Affectionately dedicated
to my wife, Jewel

Preface

*T*his book has been written with the lay reading in mind, so it is to no degree an effort to set forth in formal theological terminology the ideas contained herein. It is not intended to be an argument to substantiate these ideas presented, but rather its purpose is to share personal beliefs that the author has come to have through a ministry of forty years.

The direct, personal style of writing has been followed with this purpose in mind. Clarity and simplicity have been the aim in the method of presentation, and technical terms have been avoided wherever possible in order to meet this aim.

References to other authors are few, primarily because this is not an effort to establish or prove concepts by following the scribal method of quoting from a large number of rabbis. It should be taken for granted that no man is an island unto himself any more in his ideas and concepts of spiritual truth than he is in any other field. All of us are the results of influences that have come to us from those whom we have heard speak and whose writings we have read. So the author does not claim originality in presenting these views; however, he does assume responsibility for what he believes to be true concerning the ideas presented.

It will be noted that many Scriptures are given that, to the author, are bases for his conclusions. Three types of ideas are presented in this book. First, those that appear to the author to be direct scriptural teaching. Second, those that seemingly can be reasonably deduced from plain scriptural teaching. Third, thoughts that are the personal opinion of the author. An effort has been made to indicate which of the ideas is personal opinion. They are shared with the hope that they may suggest lines of thought that can be helpful in a fuller understanding of the entire subject. There is no effort to convince any other person that the final word has been spoken on the subject. In fact, the author believes that none of us can understand the full truth about everything. The best we can do on many of the details is to speculate.

It is hoped that much practical good can be derived from a careful reading of this book, and that God will be made more real, heaven more meaningful, and that in it all, Christ shall be magnified.

Arthur E. Travis

It's Hard to Talk about Heaven

*W*e are interested in heaven and would like to know as much as we can about it. Likely no person ever lived who did not at some time ask himself Job's question, "If a man die, shall he live again?" Our Christian faith answers that question with a strong yes. The truth is that we shall not just live again; we shall *go on living* after death. This is the Christian hope and it settles the most important of all questions we might ask about heaven. Heaven is real.

At the same time, there are many other things we would like to know about heaven. Where is it? What conditions prevail there? Shall we know each other in heaven? Will there be differences between God's children in heaven? There are dozens of questions like these. We shall seek to find the answers to as many of our questions as we can, keeping in mind that we want God's answers, not just man's speculation.

Before we begin discussing these answers, let us admit a difficulty: it is hard to talk about heaven. Just how do we discuss this subject? Likely we follow a pretty familiar line of thought and express our beliefs in words and phrases we have heard most of our lives. In all honesty, when we have said all we know, we must leave the subject feeling that "the half has not been told." Furthermore, we often feel a certain uneasiness about exploring any subject beyond what we have always assumed to be true.

We often feel as reluctant to talk about death as we do to talk about God. Many of us absolutely refuse to discuss death; we do not even want to listen to anyone else talk about it. I have known of a husband and wife who refused to discuss the fact that the wife was afflicted with a terminal disease. They preferred to ignore the fact and try to live as though everything were normal. This attitude toward talking of death often prevents a free discussion of life after death.

Others of us avoid talking about heaven because of a criticism we have heard. Some people claim that Christians are so other-worldly that they neglect to do what they should do in this life. The accusation is that Christians have a "pie-in-the-sky theology," while at the same time they are woefully lacking in serving needy people on earth. In order to disprove this accusation, we often refuse to talk about heaven at all. This extreme caution is unnecessary; it can even become hurtful in keeping us from developing our Christian hope as we should. The truth is that a right kind of thinking and talking about heaven will challenge and inspire us to do more now. There are likely some people who neglect life now because they are so engrossed in their concepts of what is in the future. However, this need not be true of any of us. We are to see our relationship with God as a whole; the present and the future are to go together. Life must have a faithful present anchored in an assured future if it is to be at its best.

As we analyze our attitudes and actions further, we find that some of our difficulty in talking about heaven is due to our preconceived ideas. We may have been told by someone who was supposed to know that we should not try to understand anything about heaven because the things of heaven have not been revealed yet. This idea is based on a misunderstanding of Paul's statement in 1 Corinthians 2:9. He wrote, "But as it is written, Eye hath not seen, nor ear heard, neither have entered into the heart of man, the things which God hath prepared for them that love him" (KJV). The misunderstanding consists of applying this statement to Christians. Paul spoke of the "rulers of this world" of verse 8. He did not say that Christians do not know anything about heaven; in fact, in verse 10, he said, "But unto us God revealed them through the Spirit." So the idea is not that we cannot know anything about heaven; it is just the opposite: God *has* revealed the truth about "the things which God hath prepared for them that love him."

We are mistaken when we refuse to discuss the things of heaven because we feel there is nothing we can know. It is true that we cannot understand *everything* about heaven, but we can come to know the things that God has revealed. The things that God has prepared for them that love him include everything involved in our salvation, now and after death. He has revealed all we need to know about life on earth as well as everything we need to know about heaven. Let us not jump to conclusions and fail to learn what God wants us to know. Furthermore, let us not be hesitant in talking about what we do know, or even in discussing what we do not know. This is one way in which we can learn more.

There is one other difficulty we shall mention; it is due to the complexity of the subject. This complexity consists of the nature of heaven itself, our own nature, and the fact that our vocabulary consists of time-space words. You have only to try to think of heaven to realize the difficulty, for as you turn your thoughts in this direction, you begin to feel yourself limited. Your earthly way of thinking colors every thought you have. Then when you try to talk about your ideas of heaven, you find your words cannot express what you feel. Yes, it is truly hard to talk about heaven.

Nevertheless, we must not allow any of these difficulties to keep us from seeking to understand as much as we can concerning our Christian hope. Although now we "see through a glass darkly," we are to look, and we are to let what we see make the difference in the way we live. Paul urged the Christians at Colossae to do this. He wrote, "Set your mind on the things that are above, not on the things that are upon the earth" (Col 3:2). He did not mean that we are to neglect living and working now in favor of daydreams about heaven. He did mean that the Christian's mind should always be heaven oriented rather than earthbound. The same truth is expressed in Paul's letter to Titus. "For the grace of God hath appeared, bringing salvation to all men, instructing us, to the intent that, denying ungodliness and worldly lusts, we should live soberly and righteously and godly in this present world; looking for the blessed hope and appearing of the great God and our Savior Jesus Christ" (2:11-13). The relation that should exist between our hope of heaven and our way of life now was made plain in 1 Corinthians 15:58. Paul wrote, "Where-fore, my beloved brethren, be ye steadfast, unmovable, always abounding in the work of the Lord, forasmuch as you know that your labor is not vain in the Lord." We are to endure hardness as a good soldier, not in order to be rewarded for what we do, but because we are good soldiers. The fact that our "labor is not in vain" should serve to inspire us to more faithful service, especially when the going gets rough.

The Christian hope is intended to be the bright spot in an otherwise dark world, and it can become this to us as we seek to know what God has revealed. This is our purpose in this book. My prayer for you is that the fears usually connected with thoughts of death, the uncertainties related with life beyond physical death, and the acute sorrow associated with the separation that death brings, may all be seen in the light of God's revealed truth. When we know the truth, the truth will set us free; let us, then, seek God's truth.

Let Us Begin Where We Are

$\mathcal{M}$ ost of us are convinced of several things about heaven, so we shall begin with these beliefs we have in common. Whatever else we may believe, we hold that heaven is real. It may be that much of our thinking about heaven takes on the nature of a dream where ideas are more fanciful than real, but heaven is not a dream; it is ultimate reality. It is a place greatly different from our material universe, and although life in heaven is of a much higher kind, it is real. Our relationship with God now is far too meaningful for us to believe that when this life is over, that relationship will become a fanciful dream without reality.

We also believe that life in heaven is a true continuation of the life we begin on earth. There will be many differences, all of which will be improvements, yet the life itself is the same life we receive when we are saved. Some of us may have the idea that eternal life begins when we leave this world and enter heaven. This is not true. Eternal life must begin wile we are on earth if it is ever to begin. There is no power in death to convey it to us, nor is there any provision for us to partake of it after death. Jesus said plainly that when we receive him into our hearts, we come to have eternal life; or to say it another way, we pass out of spiritual death into spiritual life (see John 5:24). This means that the moment we receive him, we are made alive with the life of God; this is eternal life. Physical death only releases us from this physical body; spiritual life thus released continues in heaven. In a real sense, heaven begins on earth; for human beings, there is no other place it can begin. We already have a foretaste of heaven in the eternal life we have now.

You may rest assured that at death you will not fall into a semi-conscious condition and spend eternity whirling around in a fairyland of fantasy and imagination. Paul knew that when he died he would go to be with Christ. He was torn between his desire to be with Christ and his desire to remain with his Christian friends on earth. It did not matter a great deal to him which it would be, although he knew it would be far better to go to be with Christ than to remain on earth. The main thing is that when he died he would not pass into a world of fantasy, but he would come into a relationship with Christ that was real (see Phil 1:23 ff.).

We need to be cautious at this point. In our effort to set forth the fact that life in heaven is real and is a continuation of spiritual life on earth, we are not to conclude that our *physical* life is to continue in heaven. Many people are deluded in thinking that heaven is to be an unending existence of enjoying physical pleasures as we know them on earth. Some of us have a picture in our minds of a life of luxury in heaven where we loll in the shade and sip pink lemonade from gold glasses. The fact is, we shall not live in physical bodies after death.

We may not be able to conceive of life apart from our physical bodies, yet we know that the physical body dies and is left in the grave, eventually to return to the dust of the ground. Paul explained that flesh and blood cannot enter into heaven (1 Cor 15:50). Only our redeemed spirits can live in a spiritual realm like heaven. Therefore, the life we know now as spiritual reality will continue in heaven, but we shall not need or desire the things associated with our present physical bodies, simply because we shall not possess physical bodies in heaven.

Yes, life in heaven is real. It is every bit as real as the life we have in Christ on earth and it is far richer and fuller than the spiritual life we have now. The fact that we shall be rid of our physical weaknesses and fleshly desires only adds greater value and meaning to life in heaven.

There is another idea about heaven that is evident from the general teachings in the Bible: heaven is a place of true happiness. We are to keep in mind that the idea of happiness in heaven is not to be limited to the lighter meaning of the word as we use it of life on earth. In this life we usually think of it as a sentimental or emotional feeling wherein we like the circumstances of life because they are pleasing to us. This shallow meaning of happiness depends upon the "happen-stances" of life. Happiness in heaven is of a much higher type; it derives from deeper causes and affects spiritual reality. It might be compared with our "happiest" moments on earth that are due to true spiritual experiences.

We love to speak and think of heaven as joy, peace, bliss, ecstasy, delight, contentment, rapture, jubilance, and final and total victory. We believe we are justified in describing our hope in these terms, giving to them even greater meaning than we can fully realize in this life. We derive a great deal of comfort in reading John's description of heaven in the book of Revelation, especially in chapters 21 and 22. In 22:3-4, we read: "And I heard a great voice out of the throne saying, Behold, the tabernacle of God is with men, and he shall dwell with them, and they shall be his peoples, and God himself shall be with them, and be their God: and he shall wipe away every tear from their eyes; and death shall be no more; neither shall there be mourning, nor crying, nor pain, any more: the first things are passed away."

Someone has suggested that heaven will be a place of perfect happiness because of two things: first, there will be nothing in heaven to prevent happiness; and second, heaven will have everything that is necessary to produce true happiness. Let us consider these two ideas.

There will be nothing in heaven that can prevent God's children from being supremely happy. There will not even be anything there that can interfere with our happiness. We shall be happy and we shall remain happy for eternity, for nothing can keep us from it in heaven. We might make a list of everything that could possibly rob us of true happiness or that could cause a person to be unhappy, and having done so conclude that absolutely none of these things will exist in heaven.

The basic cause of unhappiness in our lives now is a self-centered attitude. When we are unhappy in this life, it is either because we have something we do not want and cannot get rid of it, or we want something we do not have and cannot obtain it. In both cases, our problem lies in how we react toward the situation as it affects us personally. Unless we are self-centered, circumstances do not make us unhappy. When we are Christ-centered, we are happy regardless of all circumstances. In heaven our self-centered nature will no longer be present to make us unhappy. If it should be, we would still be unhappy, even in a perfect place like heaven. But in heaven we shall be completely God-centered without a selfish thought in us. Heaven will be glorious because no selfishness will exist there. The prayer of Jesus in John 17:21-23 indicates this: "That they may all be one; even as thou, Father, art in me, and I in thee, that they also may be in us. . . . And the glory which thou hast given me I have given unto them; that they may be one, even as we are one; I in them, and thou in me, that they may be perfected into one, that the world may know that thou didst send me, and lovedst them, even as thou lovedst me."

There is another way to state the same truth. There will be no sin in heaven. Sin is a destroyer of happiness; it robs the hearts of men of the very things that can make a person truly happy. John assured his readers, "There shall in no wise enter into it anything unclean, or he that maketh an abomination and a lie: but only they that are written in the Lamb's book of life (Rev 21:27). He made this truth more definite in Revelation 22:15: "Without are the dogs, and the sorcerers, and the fornicators, and the murderers, and the idolaters, and every one that loveth and maketh a lie. "We can rest assured that in a place where there will be neither sinner nor sinning, we shall know true happiness.

Lest we might think that true happiness is not dependent upon inward holiness and freedom from evil, let us remind ourselves that our happiest moments on earth have not depended upon external circumstances. Rather, we have known deepest happiness when our hearts have been in harmony with God. However, we can be assured that there will not be anything of any sort in heaven that can possibly make us unhappy. Not only will the inner things such as guilt, fears, anxieties, and the like, be forever gone, but there will be nothing to bring sorrow, heartache, or a sense of failure. As John said, there will be no more death and the separation it brings; there will be no weeping or loneliness. Nothing, absolutely nothing, will be in heaven to prevent perfect happiness.

At the same time, heaven holds everything that is necessary for the perfect happiness of God's children. The things we now think are necessary for happiness may not be in heaven, but all that is needed to produce true happiness is there in perfection and abundance. The abundant life Jesus makes possible here will be realized fully only in heaven.

The one thing above all else that will cause us as God's children to be supremely happy in heaven is the fact that we shall be in the presence of our loving heavenly Father, and we shall have unhindered fellowship with him. We were created for God. God intended for us to have a relationship with him in which he could give himself to us for our highest good. We are miserable with anything less than this harmonious relationship with our Father-Creator. In heaven this relationship will have finally become a reality without any interference, and we shall know the fullness of his holy presence.

We have indicated that oneness with God rules out self-centeredness and disharmony in heaven; now we emphasize that we shall have positive and unhindered oneness with God. Our limited experience of God's presence on earth assures us that when we get to heaven, just being with God will be the best our hearts could know.

Another aspect of this unhindered fellowship with God is the fact that in heaven God's perfect will is done. Evil exists in this world because man is disobedient to God's will, but in heaven, every thought, desire, and choice is according to the will of God. Jesus taught his disciples to pray: "Thy kingdom come. Thy will be done, as in heaven, so on earth" (Matt 6:10). He meant by "as in heaven" that his Father's will is done perfectly there and indicated that this is to be the object of our praying and living on earth. He himself was the perfect example of the Father's will in a person's life on earth. He said, "My meat is to do the will of him that sent me, and to accomplish his work" (John 4:34). Again he said, "I can of myself do nothing: as I hear, I judge: and my judgement is righteous; because I seek not mine own will, but the will of him that sent me" (John 5:30). A little later re repeated the same truth, "For I am come down from heaven, not to do mine own will, but the will of him that sent me" (John 6:38). Then he said, "And he that sent me is with me; he hath not left me alone; for I do always the things that are pleasing to him" (John 8:29). The blessedness of the Father's will was clearly manifested in the greatest life ever lived on earth, that of Jesus Christ. In heaven, the Father's will, accepted and obeyed by all, produces blessedness beyond measure. We would have more of the abundant life here and now if we would only abide in his will; in fact, we do have an abundant life to the degree that we follow his will.

In speaking of abundant life, we are reminded that in heaven, life itself will be the true Life of God, a fact that opens the way for untold joy. God's Life is eternal life; it is the only kind of life that can exist in heaven. On earth we are made alive with the life of God, but we allow so many things to interfere with God's life in us that we do not come to experience its fullness. In heaven God's Life flows full and unhindered, making it possible for us to know true life as God himself knows it and as he intended us to know it. This life, in the presence of God and in perfect harmony with his will, has everything that brings happiness. It is characterized by certain qualities.

The life of God is a life of true holiness, righteousness, and love. True goodness brings greater blessedness than all the pleasures of the world. Since life in heaven is perfect in every way, it is productive of genuine joy. True happiness is not something we find by seeking it; it is rather the natural result of what we are and do. In heaven, we shall be the kind of persons who do not just *find* happiness, but we shall *be* happy because we shall be holy. The inspired writers of the Scriptures and Christian poets have exhausted the supply of words trying to express the meaning and greatness of happiness in heaven, only to find they cannot do it justice in human language. Just as the pure holiness of God transcends our understanding, so the happiness of heaven is greater than we can fathom. We can know that they go together as tree and fruit. We also know that we shall be holy, and because we are like our heavenly Father, we shall be satisfied in that holiness.

Eternal life also contains the unique quality of true fulfillment for the human heart. The desire for fulfillment is a result of the fact that we are created in the image of God. The lack of fulfillment reflects the fact that we are less than God intended us to be in creation. The striving for fulfillment in this life will never be successful until we partake of the life of God; even then, it will not be total and complete on earth. However, this natural heart hunger will find total fulfillment in heaven. True meaning, deep fullness of reality, and a sense of infinite worth are all attributes of the wonderful life of God we shall have in heaven.

This description of the blessedness of eternal life in heaven could go on and on, for we could name every possible quality of true blessedness we know and still not mention all of them. We tend to emphasize those things we feel are important to us now, and perhaps we reflect our own heart's desires and a sense of lack in our lives. Realizing these possibilities, we would mention one other thing. We are told by those who make special studies of human nature, and our own hearts agree, that one of our deepest desires in this life is to feel that we are loved, that we have a special purpose in this world, that our existence is truly worthwhile. A total lack of these things leads to despondency and often to self-destructive despair. On the other hand, when we know that we are needed and loved, when we feel a real sense of mission, and when we find ourselves achieving something worthwhile, life takes on an entirely different meaning. We find ourselves truly happy. In heaven we shall know perfect love; we shall have the full love of God and be truly aware of its meaning; we shall be in the fellowship of creatures who are moved only by love; we shall feel and express love in all our relationships. Furthermore, we shall know the purpose and meaning of our place in God's heaven, and we shall be able to achieve our heart's desires for the glory of God.

We sometimes feel now that heaven will offer us a time and place for rest from our work, at least for a few thousand years. At least, we hope it will. We join Rudyard Kipling in the words of a poem. He wrote, "We shall rest, and faith we shall need it;/Lie down for an eon or two,/Til the Master of all good workmen/Shall set us to work anew." However, when we consider this matter more fully, we are aware that an eternity of idleness would not be true happiness. It is better to realize that we shall be happy in heaven because we are working joyously for the glory of God.

We shall know the purpose and meaning of our place in God's heaven, and we shall be able to achieve our heart's desires for the glory of God.

Let Us Take a Closer Look

*H*aving decided that heaven is a place of perfect happiness, let us consider now what kind of persons we shall be in that place. Many people have the idea that when we die, we shall become angels. This idea is perhaps developed because we naturally think of heavenly creatures as angels. The Bible often refers to angelic beings as creatures that inhabit heaven, so the idea is deduced from this that we shall become angels when we die. This is not true; we shall not become angels, for angels are a different kind of creature from men. The Bible does not give us a detailed description of angels, but we can learn something about them from the occasions in the Bible when they appeared to men, along with the qualities and activities attributed to them.

Someone has suggested that all angels were created at the same time and were placed on probation for a set time. The supposition is that they were free to choose to remain loyal to God or to reject his sovereignty during this period. Those that remained loyal became permanently holy creatures, while those that rebelled became permanently alienated from God and evil in nature. The Bible teaches that Satan is the prince of the these fallen angels; it does not indicate there is any redemptive plan for the salvation of fallen angels.

Our knowledge of man is much fuller than our knowledge about angels. We have an account of God's creation of man in which we are told that man was created in the image of God, a fact that is not attributed to angels, although since they were creatures of choice, it may be that they also were created in God's image. We are also told that man, like the fallen angels, rejected God and became a sinful creature. However, God's plan of redemption for man brings an entirely new truth into view. Through the atoning death of Jesus Christ a human soul can become a child of God. This means that we are born into God's family when we are saved and are sons of God forever. As God's children, we are greater than any other creatures in existence, including the angels of heaven. For the time being we are lower than the angels, but in heaven we shall be greater than they can ever become.

So when we die and go to heaven, we are not to become angels. There are some scriptural statements that are interpreted as teaching this, so let us consider them briefly. In Matthew 18:10, Jesus is quoted as saying, "See that ye despise not one of these little ones, for I say unto you, that in heaven their angels do always behold the face of my Father who is in heaven." Jesus did not say that children become angels, but rather that angels attend children now, evidently guarding them from harm. We may or may not conclude that each child has a guardian angel, but we can safely say that Jesus agreed with the statement in Hebrews 1:14 about angels. "Are they not all ministering spirits, sent forth to do service for the sake of them that shall inherit salvation?"

There is another statement of Jesus about angels that might be misunderstood. The Sadducees had confronted Jesus with a problem involving the resurrection of the dead and in answer to their question he explained relationships in heaven in these words, "For in the resurrection they neither marry, nor are given in marriage, but are as angels in heaven" (Matt 22:30). In saying that we shall be "as angels," Jesus did not mean that we shall actually be angels. We shall be as the angels in regard to sex; angels are not male or female, and Jesus only said that there will be no problem about marrying in heaven because there will be no male and female human beings. We shall all be children of God and sex will be no part of our nature.

Since we shall not be angels, just what kind of creatures shall we be when we get to heaven? In regard to this question John wrote these words, "Beloved, now are we children of God, and it is not yet made manifest what we shall be. We know that, if he shall be manifested, we shall be like him; for we shall see him as he is" (1 John 3:2). We shall be like Jesus; this is enough for many of us. We are satisfied to leave the entire matter right here and not try to go any further in our search. We rejoice in Paul's statement that God has ordained that all his children be "conformed to the image of his Son" (Rom 8:29), and we are assured of the fact that just as surely as we are partakers of Adam's nature now, "we shall also bear the image of the heavenly" (1 Cor 15:49), that is, we shall be like Christ in heaven.

There are others of us who rejoice in this great truth, yet we want to know more. We know that not all has been made known, but we believe a great deal more has been revealed than most of us have understood. We are interested in how much we shall know in heaven. Shall we know who and what we were on earth? Shall we know what continues to happen on earth after we are in heaven? Will there be a personal concern about our loved ones and what happens to them on earth? What will be the relationships between people in heaven? Will earthly relationships carry over into heaven?

Let us consider these questions under two headings. First, what about our knowledge? Second, what about our relationships?

A general observation about our knowledge in heaven is that we shall know as much as we know on earth and a great deal more. Paul compared our knowledge on earth with he knowledge we shall have in heaven in 1 Corinthians 13:8-12. Earthly knowledge is partial, often distorted, and will eventually pass away. He compares the knowledge and understanding of a child with that of an adult, noting that the wisdom of the adult replaces the immature understanding of the child. Even so, our knowledge and understanding in heaven will replace and surpass our knowledge now. Everything we see now is as though it were a riddle, vaguely reflected as we would behold our reflection in a besmirched mirror, but in heaven we shall see as though at close range, with unhindered vision, and without interference of any kind.

Our heavenly knowledge as characterized by Paul will be perfect and full. It will not only be knowledge in a higher degree than our earthly knowledge, but it will be a different kind. It is doubtful if we know anything on earth as it truly is. Every idea is affected by something that prevents pure and perfect understanding on our part. At best, we simply know only in part. Our knowledge in heaven will be similar to God's knowledge of us now, for, as Paul wrote, "Then shall I know fully even as also I was fully known."

We do not know how completely we shall know God. From our vantage point now we feel that for all eternity we can never exhaust the fullness of the knowledge of God. We are assured that we shall know him in all the fullness in which he has revealed himself in Christ. Jesus prayed that his followers would be with him and behold his glory. John was sure that we shall see him as he is. We conclude, therefore, that we shall know God just as fully as he can be known by his children.

Shall we know what we were and did on earth? There is no reason for us to believe that physical death will erase our earthly life from our memories. We would expect to know fully everything about our past life. We shall have a different understanding of it, but at the same time, we shall know. Jesus said that at some time, perhaps at the judgment, everything will be revealed, that nothing will remain hidden (see Luke 12:2).

One of the most interesting questions of all concerns our knowledge in heaven of what is occurring on earth. We wonder if we shall know what is happening in the lives of our loved ones who remain on earth, if their needs will still concern us, and more especially if we shall know of our earthly loved ones who are not Christians or who have died without Christ.

We should be careful in making hard-and-fast statements about these matters that we do not go beyond what the Bible reveals. We realize that many details about heaven have not been specifically explained; our conclusions on these things should be recognized as opinions. We should form our opinions on sound scriptural principles, but even then we should not be dogmatic in our conclusions.

We have already noted that we shall surely know as much in heaven as we know on earth. This knowledge will include an awareness of our past; we are not sure just how much of the continuing activities and happenings on earth we shall know. Because of the nature of this subject and the lack of specific teaching, there are differing opinions on the matter.

There are some people who believe that our loved ones in heaven are looking on the affairs of men and earth and that they are fully aware of all that is happening. This idea is drawn from the statement in Hebrews 12:1 that we are surrounded by a great cloud of witnesses. The meaning of the word "witnesses" according to this interpretation, is to look on, to see what is going on. This idea applies to spectators at a ball game; they are witnessing the game. The conclusion is reached from this word that those in heaven are thus witnessing us and our lives on earth. Because of this fact, goes the explanation, we should be faithful in our Christian life and service.

Whether those in heaven are thus witnessing events on earth may or may not be true, but this Scripture does not apply to that idea at all. The meaning of Hebrews 12:1 must be derived from what the writer was saying, for his use of the word "witness" is to be understood in the sense in which he intended it. We get this from the context which includes the entire eleventh chapter. The big question is, "Can the Christians to whom he wrote afford to give up their earthly safety, endure persecution, and undergo all that is involved in the Christian life for them with only the gospel of Christ as a basis for doing it?"

The eleventh chapter emphasizes the fact that all relationship with God must be based purely on faith, a faith in which man has only God's word for his commitment and confidence. However, there is one other factor; that factor is the example of the great people through the centuries who have committed their lives, often unto death, with nothing but faith as the basis of that commitment. They suffered greatly because of their faith, yet their faith endured and they stand as the spiritual giants of all time. They also stand to witness to the great truth that the Christians to whom the book of Hebrews was written needed above all else. That great truth is that a person *can* afford to commit himself to God in faith without reservation, for God is true. In fact, there is nothing else that is worthy of our total commitment. Because of this, the Christian can live his life, enduring all manner of opposition or persecution; he can stand true to God, patiently accepting whatever may become a part of his Christian life, knowing all the while what the ultimate outcome will be. He has both the Word of God and the experiences of those who have already proved that Word to undergird his faith. This is the meaning of the witnesses of Hebrews 12:1; thus it does not apply to the subject we are discussing.

Does this mean then that our loved ones in heaven do not know what we are doing? No, it does not mean that. This interpretation of Hebrews 12:1 simply means that the writer is not discussing that particular subject in this verse. We do not have any statements in the New Testament that specifically tell us one way or the other what is true about this matter. We might conclude from Paul's statement "we shall know fully even as we are fully known" that as God knows us now, we shall know about our loved ones when we get there. However, this interpretation is like walking on thin ice and we shall be safer simply to conclude that this question is not answered in the New Testament.

The writers of the New Testament do not discuss the details of the condition of believers in heaven between death and the resurrection except for one thing: we shall be with Christ! All else is dwarfed by this great fact. Paul's desire was to depart and be *with Christ*; nothing else seemed to concern him. He reflected the same truth in writing to the Thessalonian Christians about their loved ones who had died. They were with Christ and will be raised first when Christ returns to earth.

The best we can do is to say that we do not have any statements that tell us our loved ones do not know what we are doing. They may know; but if they do know, we can be sure they see things from a viewpoint entirely different from our earthly way of seeing things. If our loved ones in heaven know us fully even as God knows us fully, then they have a clear understanding of all that is involved and respond to it as God does.

Do Christians in heaven know about their earthly loved ones who have died and gone to hell? Jesus indicated that the rich man in hell knew about Lazarus in heaven; does this mean that Lazarus knew about the rich man? Abraham did know about him and talked with him; how much of this can we apply to our question? It has been suggested that if a Christian in heaven does know of his earthly loved one in hell, he will have the same attitude God has toward him.

It has also been suggested that the Christian in heaven will not know about those in hell. The explanation is given that a mother who might have given birth to four children but actually had only two, does not know that two that were not born. Even so, the soul in hell was never born spiritually into God's family, so just does not exist to those who have been born again. The argument is that in heaven we shall know only that which is spiritually alive, and hell with all those there will pass into outer darkness as though they had never existed.

Since there is no definite statement in the New Testament concerning this matter, we must leave it without trying to settle it one way or the other. Although we might like to have an answer to this question, it is not necessary that we have it. We can rest assured that we shall know all we need to know and that our reaction to what we shall know will be according to our Father's will. We shall likely be so filled with the glory of his presence that all these questions will not even enter our minds.

What about our earthly relationships such as husband and wife, parents and children, brothers and sisters? Will these relationships be the same in heaven as they are on earth? This is a subject that is very near our hearts for we would like to believe that we shall continue these relationships forever. Let us note two things concerning this matter.

The Christians at Thessalonica were concerned about their loved ones who had died; they feared that when Christ returned, the living would be caught up to be with him, but those who had died would be left behind in the graves. They were interested in this relationship with their loved ones.

Paul's answer (1 Thess 4:13 ff.) does not specifically say there will be a continuation of earthly relationships, yet he does say that the dead in Christ will be raised first, so they will not be left out. After that, the living will be caught up *with them* to meet the Lord in the air.

Paul placed emphasis on two things in this verse. He used a word that indicates that the raising of the dead and the transformation of the living will take place at the *same time*, which is the same as saying be together *with them*. We may be reading our wishes into this statement, but it seems that Paul indicated there will be something special about our being together with our earthly loved ones. It is evident that the major concern is that all of us will be with the Lord, yet at the same time, the other idea is in his statement. We may safely conclude that there will be special meaning for us in having our earthly loved ones *with us* to share in the glory of being in his presence.

Even though this is true, we must go on to say that we shall not have the same relationships in heaven we have on earth. We shall not be husband and wife in the same way we are in this life, nor will any other earthly relationship be the same in heaven it is on earth. Jesus made this clear when he talked with the Sadducees. Some of them came to him in an effort to prove that any idea of a resurrection at all was unthinkable. They posed the situation in which a woman was married to a man who died. The levirate law of Moses stated that the brother of the deceased man would marry the woman and rear children for him. The Sadducees suggested that this particular woman was married to seven brothers. Their problem was which of the seven brothers in heaven would have her as his wife.

They believed they had proof in this question that there is no resurrection of the dead. However, Jesus explained that this was no problem at all for the simple reason that there is no marrying in heaven (see Luke 20:34-36; Matt 22:30). He said that in heaven all will be like the angels in that there will be no sex, there will be neither male nor female. Sex is strictly a physical quality; in heaven there are no physical bodies, so there will be no sex. Men will no longer be men nor will women be women. All of God's children will be just that-children of God without physical distinctions such as sex.

We conclude from this explanation Jesus gave that our earthly relationships that are physical will no longer exist in heaven. Earthly husband and wife will not be husband and wife in heaven; parent and child on earth will not be parent and child in heaven. Even while we are on earth, we are all spiritual children of God in the same way. There is no difference spiritually between a man and a woman; our spirits are the same. When these bodies are left on earth and our spirits go to heaven, all of our physical differences will cease to exist and we shall be spiritual children without sex or earthly human relationships.

If we feel a tinge of regret that this will be true, let us not think it strange; this is normal when we deeply love our relationships on earth. This fact does make death the final end of earthly relationships, yet we are not to grieve because of this. As children of God we are to realize that our relationships in heaven will be far greater in every way than even the best we have known on earth. The closest relationship any husband and wife have enjoyed on earth will become perhaps a sweet memory in heaven, but will be totally eclipsed by the glory of new relationships there.

God never allows his children to lose anything of value that is not replaced with something far greater as we follow his will and enter into what he has prepared for us. Our greatest rejoicing in heaven as it relates with any earthly relationships we have had will consist in a mutual elation in sharing the glory and presence of Christ.

To be in his presence will be heaven; to be in his presence with our earthly loved ones may make heaven a bit sweeter, but heaven will not depend on these former earthly relationships. Our hearts will be filled with a love for God and all his children that will overshadow all earthly loves. There is nothing in this to detract from heaven; there is everything to make it more glorious. On earth husband and wife have come into a relationship that far exceeds the physical; as Christians, their hearts beat as one in their love of Christ. In heaven the relationship will be far better.

A Good Look at Ourselves

*W*e have said in the last chapter that the center of heaven for a Christian is Jesus Christ. To be in his presence will captivate the heart of all of God's children. Let us keep this in mind as we turn our attention to ourselves, lest we think we shall be self-centered there. We shall have no particle of selfish pride in us when we get to heaven. However, we do need to understand from a positive point of view what kind of persons we shall be.

We shall be individual persons, retaining our own identities. We shall have a unity unrealized on earth, yet at the same time, it will be a unity of individuals with each one a true person and all in harmony with God and with one another. We shall know who and what we are, and perhaps of more importance, why we are that kind of individual. God created man as an individual and intended for him to remain a person for eternity. He respects man's freedom and always will respect it. In heaven we shall freely and fully choose to be in perfect harmony with God and thereby come into a realization of true personhood. We shall be as truly a person as we are now.

Jesus said that God is the God of Moses and Elijah. This is equal to saying that Moses and Elijah are still Moses and Elijah; they have not ceased being individuals. Moses died a physical death, yet he continues to be Moses in heaven. The idea that we shall all melt into an impersonal whole and lose our identity as persons is not founded on scriptural teaching.

The gist of what we are saying is that you will still be you, a real live person, knowing as a person and known as a person. It is this person we seek to understand. What can we say about our characteristics as a person in heaven? We have already noted that our eternal life must begin on earth, that the spiritual life that begins at conversion will continue in heaven, so the very same person we have become during our earthly life is the person we shall be in heaven. In physical

death we are set free from our carnal nature and the limitations we have while in our physical bodies, but the person we
have become as a child of God will be the person we are in
heaven. There is no power in death to transform us from a
lost soul into a child of God and there is no power in death to
transform us from a spiritually immature child into a full-
grown spiritual adult.

We may have difficulty with this idea if we have not
considered it before now, so let us discuss it more fully. One
of the major aspects of Christian truth and experience is that
when we become a Christian, we become a new creation.
When we repent and exercise saving faith, God regenerates
our spirit, making us an entirely new kind of human being.
Thy physical body is not changed; the carnal nature remains
to contend for our lives, but we actually become a different
person. This experience is spoken of as being born again, so
we begin our Christian life as a spiritual baby. We are capable
of spiritual growth, we are admonished to grow, and we have
at our command all that is necessary for spiritual growth. In
spiritual growth we become a person of maturity. It is not so
much that we learn what to be and how to be what we need
to be, but rather that in learning and responding, we actually
become more Christlike.

It is not difficult for us to realize that people as we know
them now are in varying stages of spiritual maturity. It is not
our place to judge or categorize the other person, yet we can
recognize the fact that there are differences between people
according to spiritual maturity. The point of what we are
saying now is that the person we become during this life, the
person we are at physical death, is the very same person we
shall be in heaven.

You might well ask the question, "Where is this idea
taught in the Bible?" My answer is that, so far as I know,
there is no specific statement of the concept. Frankly, the conclusion is arrived at from reasoning and the application of
basic principles in the Bible. In instances like this, there is
always the possibility of being wrong, so we must avoid dog-
matism in our conclusions. However, there is no statement or

principle in the Bible that either presents an alternative or that forbids this conclusion. Let us follow the line of reasoning that has led me to this belief.

When the mother of James and John came to Jesus to ask that her sons be given the highest places of honor in the new kingdom, Jesus told her and the two young men, "My cup indeed ye shall drink: but to sit on my right hand, and on my left hand, is not mine to give; but it is for them for whom it hath been prepared of my Father" (Matt 20:23). It is clear that Jesus spoke of a principle by which the Father determines matters like this. God does not do his work by arbitrary decisions; he always works according to principles that are righteous and just. There are certain things, like position and rewards in heaven, that are determined according to these principles.

At another time, Jesus told his disciples, "Unto you it is given to know the mysteries of the kingdom of heaven, but to them it is not given" (Matt 13:11). The subject we are discussing would be considered a true mystery of the kingdom. Our problem now is this: What is the principle, or mystery, by which God determines these things?

The answer is that the general principle lies in the area of cause and effect. Certain things either bring about certain effects, or they make it possible for effects to be produced. Salvation is the gift of God, yet it is not effective for any particular individual until that person receives it. The condition for God's exercise of saving power is man's attitude and spirit of repentance and faith manifested and expressed. In a similar way, the condition for spiritual growth is the individual's partaking of those things God has provided for that spiritual growth. If he does not partake, then he does not grow; if he does not grow, then he is not mature. There is no indication in the Bible that God has arranged for any method by which a human soul can grow except through this general principle. One of the great truths in the New Testament concerning this life is that we are *to become* what we need to be. This aspect of our Christian faith is central; everything else hinges on our becoming. The primary concern is not what we do, but what we become. We first become, then we do. To carry the truth further, we cannot be what we do not become; it is equally true that *what* we become, the kind of person we become from every viewpoint, we are.

The importance of this idea of becoming is seen in the fact that the word used in the New Testament for "become" is found over six hundred times. It is given forty different shades of meaning in the translations, but there is always the idea of coming to be or something coming about, either in the process or result. We might paraphrase the teaching as it applies to our problem: "*Get to be*, because you will be what you come to be." This is certainly true in this life; I believe it is also true that what we become in this life, we shall be in heaven. You might well ask yourself just what kind of person you are right now from a spiritual viewpoint, the real you. If you should die now, you would enter into heaven the very same spiritual person you are now.

Does this mean that Christians will be different in heaven just as they are different in spiritual maturity in this life? It does mean that they will be different. We have no difficulty in recognizing the differences between people in this life concerning their spiritual maturity; why should we find it strange that physical death has no power to change them? Let us remember that all of God's children will be true children of God and will share the same eternal life, but we shall not be of the same spiritual stature.

How will this affect us and our enjoyment of heaven? Shall we recognize the differences in heaven? If so, will these differences produce jealousy and a spirit of competition? Let us consider these matters briefly.

What effect will our spiritual maturity or lack of it have on us in heaven? We might find an answer in thinking of what spiritual maturity means to us in this life. One of the differences between immaturity and true spiritual maturity is in the ability to understand, to appreciate, and to enjoy the things of God.

Immature persons derive as much from the things of God as they are capable of experiencing, yet these things do not hold as deep a meaning for them as for mature Christians. Someone has illustrated it as a matter of capacity. The reference is made to two different containers, one holds a pint while the other is a gallon container. Both of them can be as full as each can be, yet the gallon container holds eight times as much as the pint container holds. All such illustrations break down if carried too far, yet there is helpful truth in this illustration. A person trained in music derives far more enjoyment from music than is possible for one who has no training in the finer points of music. The same thing is true in almost every area of learning and experience. Thus it is not strange at all that different people in heaven will be different, nor is it contrary to what we know about heaven to believe that these differences will make a difference.

The question was asked, "Shall we recognize these differences?" We recognize them here on earth; why should we not be aware of them in heaven? We shall know fully even as we are known; this will surely include this kind of knowledge.

What will our reactions be to the fact that we may be spiritually immature and incapable of enjoying heaven as much as some others enjoy it? Shall we feel jealousy toward those who are more mature? Certainly there will be no spirit of jealousy or competition among God's children in heaven. Each of us will be personally devoted to God and what any other fellow servant of God may be or do will not affect us adversely. We shall be as happy as we are capable of being and this means that we shall be happy that God has children who praise and glorify him even though they may do so in a more glorious way than we are capable of doing. All our petty and selfish attitudes and reactions will have perished when our carnal nature ceases to exist and only wholesome and holy feelings will fill our spirits.

Even in this life we recognize that many others are more spiritually mature than we are. We do not feel jealous of them for we recognize that we are as spiritually mature as we have chosen to be and the fact that others are more so only causes us to admire them and rejoice in the fact that they have become what they are. We likely have desires to be the kind of Christian we believe someone else to be, but we are not envious of his spiritual growth, for we know how he got that way and we also know that the same way is open to us, so we do not blame him; we have only ourselves to blame. In heaven we shall rejoice in all good things; the fact that many of God's children are mature will be good, so we shall be happy about that fact.

Since we shall be translated into heaven at physical death as the same person we have become during life on earth, will we be able to grow after we get to heaven? Shall we have an opportunity in heaven to become what we failed to become while on earth? We are inclined to say that since this earthly life is the time and place for new beginnings, we shall go to heaven as the person we have become and shall continue as the same person for eternity. From what we can understand of life and death, physical death crystallizes everything. On this side of death there is change; we can become what we have not been. When death once comes, however, we enter into the after-life without possibility for further changes. This idea gives added meaning and importance to our earthly existence. This life is a once-for-all affair; once we have lived, we never have another opportunity to do it again, and what we become as we live we shall forever be. If any scriptural truth to the contrary exists, this writer does not know of it.

There is the possibility that what we have begun during our earthly life will increase in heaven. This possibility is seen in one translation of a statement in the book of Revelation. John wrote, "He that is unrighteous, let him do unrighteousness still: and he that is filthy, let him be made filthy still: and he that is righteous, let him do righteousness still; and he that is holy, let him be made holy still" (Rev 22:11). This translation substantiates what has just been said. The word translated "still" usually carries the meaning when applied to time of a continuing condition, such as "What has been *still is*." This is the meaning given this word in this verse. However, the word is also used to convey the idea of "yet more." This is the marginal reading in the American Standard Version given the word. If it should have this meaning, then John said that righteousness and holiness would continue "yet more." This allows for the idea that when a person has begun in this life will increase in heaven.

We might conclude that we shall grow in heaven in the things we have begun on earth, but we shall not be able to begin something that was not begun during our life on earth. This principle is in harmony with all we know about spiritual matters and at the same time is consistent with what we believe about stewardship responsibility. The person who uses well what is entrusted to him will have more entrusted to him. This principle is not so much the idea that we are paid for what we do; it is more a natural succession of becoming and being. What a person learns, that he knows; what he trains himself to do well, that he can do well; what he becomes, that he is. Jesus urged the right attitudes on his disciples because of this truth (Luke 16:9-13). He did not specifically name the idea we speak of now, but the principle he taught includes the entire range of human experience.

Let us state it this way. God's grace has provided for our salvation. This means that he freely gives us eternal life and he gives it to all alike. There is no way or means by which we can earn or deserve forgiveness and new life; we simply commit ourselves to him and he makes us alive with his own life. However, the moment we become children of God, our life stewardship begins. This means that although God himself sustains us in our spiritual life, at the same time a great deal of the details of that spiritual life are dependent on our reactions and responses to him. We shall have more to say later about the processes of this growth in God's grace, but for now our emphasis is on the fact that what we become is our responsibility and is not an automatic working of God irrespective of what we do, but his working is in proportion to our working, never contrary to it.

Our purpose now is to apply this principle to the matter of our becoming a certain kind of person. By God's grace we do become what we are as a person. It is true that we could never become anything worthwhile without God's working, but at the same time, our spiritual growth is not automatic.

This is a foregone conclusion. When we apply the same principle to our going from this life into heaven, we realize that spiritual maturity is not accomplished by the process of physical death. Furthermore, it is no more automatic in this changing of places of existence than it is in our life on earth. This is the process through which we have arrived at the conclusion that the person we become during our life on earth is the person we shall be in heaven.

We must not become so emotionally involved in how we feel now about this idea that we misunderstand it. We are not saying that we shall not undergo any changes when we die and go to heaven. It is evident that our physical bodies will be left behind. This means that all physical qualities we now have will cease to exist at death. Paul stated that flesh and blood cannot inherit the kingdom of God. Since this is true, everything that derives from flesh and blood must be included in his statement. No fleshly desires, inclinations, needs, weaknesses, limitations-none of them will any longer be a part of our person. Thus, when we say that we shall be the same person in heaven we were at the time of death, we exclude all physical qualities of our life now.

We feel that we are equally safe in saying that all the qualities of our fallen human nature will cease to exist when we die physically. Paul used terms like the lusts of the flesh, carnal, fleshly, and the old man, in speaking of this aspect of the human being in this world. He said that the Christian is constantly beset by the desires and demands of this carnal nature (see Gal 5:16-25 for his discussion of this subject). Our purpose now is to explain that in heaven we shall no longer have this quality of our being that is naturally set against God and for self.

In our conversion experience we declare the old sinful man to be dead and ourselves no longer under his dominion. However, he refuses to die, and lives on to oppose everything we would do for God. We rejoice in the fact that when we die physically, this carnal nature will cease to be a part of our being. We shall no longer have any desire to exalt self; we shall not have fleshly desires controlling our thoughts and demanding indulgence. Instead of having to face this battle we constantly wage in this life, we shall be perfectly free to center all our interest and attention on Jesus Christ.

There will be differences in what we are now and what we shall be in heaven and these differences will make heaven a heavenly place. However, it still holds true that the kind of person each of us has become at the time of his death in the sense of spiritual maturity will be the exact person he will be in heaven. Physical death will only mean the end of all that is evil; it will set us free from earthly and human limitations, but it will not make us spiritually what we have failed to become during life on earth.

There are two questions we must answer at this point. First, what about the person who is saved near the end of his life, or even on his deathbed? What about the thief on the cross, and others with similar experiences? Will they enter heaven only spiritual babes in Christ? If we are true to the principles we find in the Bible, we must conclude that what any of these have not become in the sense of spiritual maturity, they will not be in heaven. These principles are not altered; God is no respecter of persons, so we must conclude that those who are not converted until late in life and who do not become mature will enter into heaven as the same spiritual person they were at death. They will be children of God and will enjoy heaven just as fully as they are capable of enjoying it, but they will not be what they could have been if they had been saved early in life and had spent a lifetime growing spiritually. They will not be unhappy because of this; they will simply be different from what they might have been.

If this seems to be contrary to what we would like for things to be, let us consider seriously the significance of personal freedom that is always inseparably linked with personal responsibility. The most serious factor in our lives gathers around the freedom God has given us and the results of our use of that freedom. God respects our freedom and will never force any decision upon us contrary to our own choice. This includes our use of freedom in relating with him. He will no more make us what we refuse to become as his children than he will force a lost soul to become a believer. He will save us by grace the moment we commit ourselves to him, but he cannot save us *until* we make that commitment. He will enable us to grow just as much and just as long as we open ourselves to the inflow of his grace, yet he will not force us to grow contrary to our responding to him. An unalterable principle of human existence is that we are the kind of person we become. The other side of this is that we cannot be what we do not become.

The other question concerns babies and their status in heaven. There is not much teaching in the New Testament on this subject. The statements of Jesus about little children emphasize the qualities of a little child on earth rather than being comments on the condition of children in heaven. Mark gives one statement in the words "Suffer the little children to come unto me; forbid them not; for to such belongeth the kingdom of God" (10:14). The marginal reading of the words "to such" is "of such." There is no way we can know for sure whether he meant to say that the kingdom of God consists of little children or that those in God's kingdom are like the little child in certain ways. It is likely true that he sought to get men to see that the childlike qualities of a little child, such as reality, simplicity, wholeheartedness, trust, and the like, are to characterize God's children. The adult is to become like a little child in his heart attitude toward God, for God's kingdom is made up of this kind of people. If this is what Jesus said, then we do not derive anything from this teaching concerning the status or condition of babies beyond death when they die in infancy.

What shall we say concerning babies who die before they come to the time when they can decide their relationship with God for themselves? The same questions applies to those who are born without the ability to determine moral matters: what about the mentally incompetent at death? Do they go to heaven? If so, what is their spiritual status? Are they spiritual babies? Will they continue to be babies?

I do not know of any scriptural statements that will give us any light on these questions. The best we can do is to find our answers by reasoning from what we know about God and his ways of dealing with human beings. We know that he is holy and just, therefore, we conclude that he always deals justly and rightly. We believe that God's justice means that he does not hold a person accountable for anything he has not chosen for himself in the realm of moral responsibility. Therefore, a baby is not morally responsible to God until he is old enough to make his own decision concerning his relationship with God. If the innocent baby should die before he is old enough to make this decision, then he is somehow cared for by the grace of God. This means that when a baby dies before he comes to the age of accountability, he goes to heaven.

The best explanation I have found concerning this was in a book I read years ago; I do not recall the title. The explanation claimed that the moment an innocent baby dies, God transforms it spiritually and gives it eternal life. This of course, is based on Christ's death and life-giving power. This is the best we can do with this matter. It is in harmony with everything we know about God and makes adequate provision for the salvation of the innocent human soul. The Bible does not reveal any other solution to the situation. There are other human solutions, but none of them is as much in harmony with general biblical teachings as this.

The question concerning whether or not the spirit of a baby grows after it reaches heaven is still unanswered. We can only observe that what we have said about the growth of all Christians in heaven applies equally to the spirit of the baby or the person who is mentally incompetent. We cannot be sure that God does not have a place and purpose in heaven for those who have not had an opportunity to grow spiritually during their lifetime on earth. We feel sure that he has made ample provision for all these matters, and since we are not given detailed descriptions of them in the Bible, we conclude that we can safely leave them to God's loving purposes. He will do what is right in every case.

What about Rewards in Heaven?

*L*et us review our line of thought before we consider the matter of rewards. We are thinking about the status of God's children in heaven and thus far, we have said that two things will characterize us there. First, as children of God we shall all share the life of God alike. In this respect we shall be the same kind of persons living in the same heaven. Second, each of us will be the same person in spiritual stature he became during his life on earth, and just as we are different now in spiritual maturity, we shall be different in heaven.

A third factor that will affect our condition in heaven is the matter of rewards for Christian service. This is likely a subject that most of us have not heard discussed as fully as we would like. Most of what we believe is based on traditional hearsay handed down from one generation to another and we have very little scriptural basis for any of it. Or it may be that our ideas on this subject have grown out of what we hope will be true, so our own desires dictate our beliefs. We are not surprised to find conflicting ideas on this subject.

Some people insist that there will be no differences at all between people in heaven. They believe that all of us will be exactly the same in every respect; as a result, they reject any idea of rewards for service. There are other people who admit that rewards are taught in the Bible, but they do not believe they will make any difference in people in heaven.

Some people even claim that the entire idea of rewards for service is unchristian. They say that if service is rendered with an eye to rewards, it ceases to be Christian service. This is certainly true, but it is also true that a Christian may perform service with a different purpose from that of getting rewards and be rewarded for that service. At least, the Bible contains a great deal of teaching on the subject of rewards for service. The Christian is assured that the right kind of service will be rewarded and he is encouraged to be faithful in service because of this fact. We shall mention a number of these teachings and seek some practical truths to be drawn from them.

In the Beatitudes of the Sermon on the Mount (Matt 5:10-12) Jesus spoke of the blessedness that characterizes those who suffer persecution because of their relationship with him. He said more about this particular matter than he said about any of the other "blesseds" of this series. Then he urged them to rejoice greatly when they were persecuted and gave as the reason for this rejoicing that their reward in heaven would be great. We conclude several things from this statement. Christians will be rewarded; some will be rewarded in a greater way than others, and undergoing persecution for Christ's sake will bring greater rewards than some other things will bring. It is important to note that he urged the fact of greater rewards as a basis for rejoicing. Evidently, there is something about rewards in heaven that is altogether right, and Christians are to rejoice because of this hope of rewards.

Jesus said in Matthew 16:27, "For the son of man shall come in the glory of his Father with his angels; and then shall he render unto every man according to his deeds." As we shall show later, the idea of rewards is illustrated in three parables which Jesus spoke: the parables of the vineyard workers, of the talents, and of the pounds. Paul wrote in Romans 2:6, "who shall render to every man according to his works." Again, in Romans 14:12, Paul stated, "So then each one of us shall give account of himself to God," with the idea that accounting is related with the judgment day. In 2 Corinthians 5:10 he made it clearer, "For we must all be made manifest before the judgment-seat of Christ; that each one may receive the things done in the body, according to what he hath done, whether it be good or bad." The idea back of the "for" here is, "Wherefore also we make it our aim, whether at home or absent, to be well-pleasing unto him." Thus Paul said that his belief in receiving something according to what he had done in the body was an incentive to faithfulness to Jesus Christ. 1 Corinthians 15:58 strongly urges this truth: "Wherefore, my beloved brethren, be ye steadfast, unmovable, always abounding in the work of the Lord, forasmuch as ye know that your labor is not vain in the Lord." There is an equally strong statement in Ephesians 6:6-8, "not in the way of eye service, as men pleasers; but as servants of Christ, doing the will of God from the heart; with good will doing service, as unto the Lord, and not unto men: knowing that whatsoever good thing each one doeth, the same shall he receive again from the Lord, whether he be bond or free." In Colossians 3:24-25 Paul made a similar statement: "Knowing that from the Lord ye shall receive the recompense of the inheritance: ye serve the Lord Christ. For he that doeth wrong shall receive again for the wrong that he hath done: and there is no respect of persons." Paul wrote in 1 Corinthians 3:8, "Each man shall receive his own reward according to his own labor."

There are several statements in the book of Revelation that present the same truths as these we have just read. In 22:12 we read, "Behold, I come quickly; and my reward is with me, to render to each man according as his work is." Then in 2:10 there is the statement that was written to encourage those under persecution to hold on in faith, "Be thou faithful unto death, and I will give thee the crown of life."

These are only some of the outstanding teachings on the subject of rewards for Christian service. They are enough to assure us of several things about rewards. For one thing, there is to be a direct relation between earthly service and rewards in heaven. The rewards are to be *according to his deeds* in the words of Jesus. This could hardly mean anything other than the fact that the Christian will receive rewards on the basis of his service on earth. Then it is clear that each individual is to be rewarded as an individual and according to his own works. Rewards are to come to each one as a person; Paul said, "That each one may receive the things done in the body." Our rewards for service will be as personal and distinct as they can be.

Furthermore, the fact that we are to be rewarded is urged as an incentive to faithfulness in Christian service. This does not mean that we are to serve God with the selfish purpose of profiting from that service. It does mean that we can know that as we commit ourselves to God in service, even though it may be costly, we do it in confidence that God will not fail. Paul encouraged the Corinthian Christians to faithful service with the fact that their service would not be in vain; we conclude that this is right.

Because of the emphasis in the New Testament on rewards for Christian service, we cannot agree that it is wrong to believe we shall be rewarded for our service to Christ. We should not serve for that purpose if we think of rewards as somehow benefitting us personally. It seems likely in the light of the emphasis placed on our hope of rewards in the New Testament that rewards will be of such nature that we can be thoroughly Christian and still serve with that hope in mind. We shall discuss the meaning of rewards later, but for now we leave the matter with the conclusion that rewards are real and are to be bestowed upon God's children according to their faithful service.

The idea that we are to be rewarded *according* to our service raises another question. What will be the basis of our rewards? Are we to be rewarded in proportion to how much service we have rendered, or will it be on some other basis? We know that each of us had different abilities; some of us are capable of one thing, others of us can do much more. If we are to be rewarded on the basis of how much we do, then some of us have an advantage over others. There must be a basis for determining rewards that is fair for all. Let us try to discover what that basis is.

As we study the statement in the New Testament with a view to discovering an answer concerning the basis of rewards for service, we find one thing standing out above all others. It is the matter of faithfulness over what has been entrusted to our use. Jesus frequently spoke of faithfulness as the key quality of stewardship and said that it is the final test for commendation for service. Paul noted that it is required in a steward that he be found faithful. Moses is compared with Jesus by the writer of Hebrews in that both were faithful to God in the work given them to do.

This principle is clearly illustrated in three parables Jesus spoke as we have already pointed out. Let us now study these parables. The general rule for interpreting a parable is that it was spoken with one main idea in mind. The parable itself is a familiar experience given in detail, but its purpose is usually to illustrate one unfamiliar spiritual idea. We are not to interpret parables as though they were allegories. An allegory is a made-up story in which each detail of the story is intended to illustrate its own particular truth. The parables of the talents, the pounds, and the vineyard workers all illustrate the sam spiritual truth. That truth is the answer to our question, "What is the basis of reward for Christian service?" All three parables agree in the truth illustrated.

From a logical viewpoint, three things are always involved in the matter of stewardship and service; these are, first, the matter of what is given and the opportunity for its use. Second, the steward's faithfulness in the use of what is entrusted to him; that is, the manner in which he took what was given him and took advantage of his opportunity to use it for the benefit of his master. Third, there is the matter of the reward that is given to the steward by the master. The three parables of Jesus we are considering all have these things in common. All of them were spoken to clarify this matter of the basis of rewards for service. The chart given here will provide us a graphic method of comparing these parables.

The Parable	Entrustment	Faithfulness	Reward
Vineyard Workers	Unequal	Equal	Equal
Talents	Unequal	Equal	Equal
Pounds	Equal	Unequal	Unequal

When we study this chart by comparing and contrasting the ideas expressed in the words "equal" and "unequal," we discover the truth Jesus illustrated in the parables. Simply stated, it is this: rewards are determined by the servant's faithful use of his entrustment, that is, his abilities and opportunities to use his abilities. Suppose we look at each of the parables in the light of the chart above.

First, in the parable of the vineyard workers, it is evident that all of the workers had the ability to harvest grapes.

However, they were not all given the same opportunity to use that ability. Some of them were not given an opportunity to work until late in the day. The implication is that they would have worked all day had they been hired earlier. Because of this element of equal faithfulness on the part of all the workers, they were all paid the same amount of wages. We must take this matter of faithfulness over opportunity into account in this parable or we shall make the mistake of believing that all Christians will be rewarded equally regardless of all else.

The second parable is that of the talents. In this case, the master gave unequal amounts of money to his servants, whereas in the parable of the vineyard workers it was unequal opportunity. Thus we conclude that the entrustments in stewardship include both ability and opportunity. With the stewards of the talents who received reward for their service, both were equally faithful. That is, the man to whom five talents had been given returned to his master ten talents, while the man to whom two talents had been given returned four. The ratio of increase is the same. As a result, both faithful men were rewarded in the same words. Here again it is equal faithfulness, equal rewards. We do not include the unfaithful servant in the comparison; if we should do that, the principle would be the same.

In the third parable, that of the pounds, each man was given one pound, so their entrustment and opportunity were equal in each case. Again, if we include only those who received rewards, the reward was based upon faithfulness. One of the men traded with his one pound and increased it to ten pounds. His master placed him over ten cities as his reward. The second man came to his stewardship accounting with five pounds; consequently, he was placed over five cities. His reward was in proportion to his faithfulness. These two men had not been equally faithful, so they were not equally rewarded.

One of the cautions we must take in interpreting a parable is that we do not base our doctrines strictly on our interpretation of the parable. However, the principle is that God will reward his children for service on the basis of what he has entrusted to their use in the light of their opportunity to use it. In other words, faithfulness in service will be the basis of rewards for that service. This principle is in harmony with all other scriptural teachings, so we are on safe ground in interpreting these three parables as we have. It is pretty clear also that the one main idea Jesus illustrated in each of these parables is this matter of the basis of rewards for Christian service.

Thus when we read that each person will be rewarded *according* to his own works, we can understand that the meaning is that we shall receive rewards for Christian service on the basis of what has been entrusted to us, and our opportunity to use that entrustment, or more simply stated, how faithful we have been as stewards. This is a great principle and we need to understand it clearly. Jesus said: "Who then is the faithful and wise servant, whom his lord hath set over his household, to give them food in due season? Blessed is that servant, whom his lord when he cometh shall find so doing" (Matt 24:45-46). The "blessedness" will come to those who are faithful and wise.

Because of the importance of this principle, let us analyze it further for a clearer understanding. The world judges success on the basis of how much money we make or how high in the world we may go; usually it is strictly on the basis of how much. The matter of what a person had to begin with or the opportunities that came his way is not considered by a materialistic culture. God does not evaluate men or their service on this worldly basis. Isaiah noted that God's ways are not our ways, and here is a classic example of the difference. God knows what has been given us in the way of abilities; he knows the opportunities we have; he knows in detail what we can do, and determines what we *should* do on the basis of these things. The final amount of the service we render is not the determining factor with God; he always takes account of what we do in the light of what we are able to do. There could not be a fairer basis for determining rewards for Christian service than this.

The person who has been given only one ability and who uses that ability faithfully will be rewarded as greatly as the person of equal faithfulness in his use of a dozen abilities. The fact is that in this matter of faithfulness in Christian service, all of God's children have equal opportunity. A person with limited ability is as free to exercise what he has in faithfulness as in the person with multiple abilities. It might even be more simple for him to concentrate on the one than it is for a person to be faithful in five talents. To say the least, limited ability is no excuse for not being faithful in what we do have. We can know for sure that God knows what we can do and that the rewards that come to us will be on the fair and just basis of our very own personal stewardship faithfulness.

There is a further important aspect in the matter of faithfulness. We might make the mistake of determining faithfulness on the basis of how *much* we do. It is true that in the parables of the talents and the pounds Jesus speaks of the amount of money that was returned to the master. However, we must keep in mind that a parable is a story that is true to common experience, but that each detail is not to be applied allegorically to some particular spiritual truth. Having understood the main truth that rewards are based upon faithfulness in service, we are not justified in tearing the parable apart and making it the basis for further conclusions drawn from details in the story.

Faithfulness is more a quality of character than anything else. A person may even produce large amounts of returns and still not be truly faithful in service to God. Only a faithful person can render faithful service. Faithfulness includes attitudes as well as actions. God looks on the heart, not just on the amount produced. Jesus referred to the faithful servants as *good* servants, and this was not just because they had produced more. A good servant is also a faithful servant, but he is good before he is faithful and he is faithful because he is good.

The importance of this quality of faithfulness needs to be realized. Jesus stated the principle that a person who is faithful in a little will also be faithful in much. The reason is that he is a faithful person. The amount of entrustment does not matter to a faithful person; he is as good a steward over little things as he is over big things. In fact, to a faithful heart, there are no bigs and littles between him and God. All of life is big; every entrustment is important. He is as faithful in one thing as he is in another. He is faithful, so does not need his master looking on demanding good work. He works faithfully because he is a faithful worker.

We are not surprised to read that Jesus said the person who has been faithful in the little will be given more responsibility. This is quite often true even in this world. It is true in Christian service in this world as a rule. God uses those who have become faithful servants. It has been said that if you want a job done rightly, find a man who is already busy working. This is because the busy man is usually the faithful man and the fact that he is faithful will make him a good worker in whatever he undertakes. Since these things are true in the world we know, we should not be surprised that God will reward his children in heaven on the basis of their faithfulness on earth.

It is good even now for us to realize that God does not require us to be successful as the world counts success. He simply expects us to receive what he entrusts to us, to give our honest effort in faithful service, and to know that a faithful heart in loving, obedient service is all he expects. Wherefore, let the one-talented person, the person with limited opportunities, the person in an out-of-the-way place of service, the person who never receives worldly acclaim, take heart; for God will reward each person, not according to the fanfare the world has given, not according to the degree of fame each has attained, not according to the millions of dollars he has garnered, but altogether according to the faithfulness of the heart and life in the light of his God-given abilities and opportunities. God could not be fairer; he will be this fair.

Will All Good Works Be Rewarded?

*W*ill the Christian receive a reward for every service he has rendered that can be classified as "good works"? At first thought one might answer, "Yes, he will." In the light of what we have said in the previous discussion, we might conclude that the one and only basis for rewards is faithfulness. However, when we study the matter more closely, we discover that this is not true. As we have noted, faithfulness will be the basis of reward, yet this does not mean that the only matter involved in rewards is faithfulness, unless of course, we include in faithfulness these other qualities. The Bible indicates clearly that there is much religious work or service that will not be rewarded.

The fullest and clearest teaching on this aspect of our subject is found in Paul's discussion in 1 Corinthians 3:10-15. In the earlier verses of this chapter Paul has commented on the carnal nature of the Corinthian Christians as evidenced by the fact that they were torn by jealousy and strife and were divided into cliques, some following one man while others followed another. He went on to discuss the place of men as leaders in God's kingdom; all of them are simply stewards of God, serving in the capacity God has assigned to each. Although all these men were servants of God alike, yet each of them would be rewarded individually according to his own work. From this fact Paul drew the conclusion that the work of a servant of God can be compared with a building. There is only one true foundation for all buildings that are considered true buildings of God; that foundation is Jesus Christ. However, the building itself consists of the service that is rendered by the individual person, and these buildings differ according to the kind of material put into them. Paul used six words in describing the kind of building material a servant of God may use in his life of service: gold, silver, costly stones, wood, hay, stubble. He went on to state that the building of each person is to be tried by fire; that is, the testing of the material in the building will be, so to speak, subjected to fire. This fire will be God's evaluation of its worth. Some buildings will come through this testing and the builder will receive reward for his service; other buildings will be consumed by the fire, and that builder will not be rewarded, but will lose his efforts expended in the service.

It is not difficult to recognize in the six words Paul used that there are only two different kinds of building materials man can use. The gold, silver, and precious stones are of such nature that they will withstand fire and come through purified, while the wood, hay, and stubble will be consumed by the fire and leave only ashes. We conclude there are two kinds of service men can render as servants of God. They are first, the kind of service that will be rewarded, and second, the kind of service that will not be rewarded.

It is true that Paul used this illustration primarily in speaking of the leaders in the churches, yet we know that God deals with all men after the same principles, so we have no hesitancy in applying the teaching here to all Christians. The big question is this: what makes the difference in Christian service? Paul said that "the fire itself shall prove each man's work of what sort it is." We conclude that there are different *sorts* of service; we would like to know what makes the difference. What must be true of our good works, our church work, our building material, if it is to be gold, silver, or precious stones? To state it another way, what qualities of heart and work does God accept as pleasing service? The very fact that these things can be likened to wood, hay, or stubble, tells us that people can render service that is not acceptable with God. Let us see if we can discover the qualities of Christian service that will stand the test.

We begin with the basic principle that God does not determine the value of things according to human standards. Men consider the externals, perhaps the efficiency or perfection of the action itself, but God places the greater value on the heart of the worker. Two people may perform a similar service wherein one of them does an excellent job as men see it while the other rather botches up his work. God may richly bless the person with the botched up work and count the work of the other absolutely worthless. Or it could be that two people do practically the same kind of work so far as men can detect, but God will reward one of them wile the work of the other is only stubble in God's evaluation. This is not because God does not value excellent work, for he does. It certainly does not mean that he places a premium on shoddy work. It does mean that he determines the value of service by something other than the act itself.

The truth is that God evaluates everything a person does by the person himself. Man's heart must be right with God before anything he does is acceptable. "But," someone will say, "isn't a Christian right with God in his heart?" Yes, he is right in his basic relationship, yet there are several aspects of his service that may be other than what they should be. A Christian may be wrong and do wrong even though he is reconciled with God in his heart. Otherwise, he would never commit sin. Just as truly as he can commit sin, he can render service in a wrong way. "All right," someone else will say, "tell us what the difference is between gold service and wood service."

There are three things that determine the quality of service Christians can render. I do not mention them in any order of importance; all of them are essential if the service is to be of the sort that will endure the testing by fire.

First, the heart motive of the worker must be right. That is, he must be moved to render the service by the right motivation. Here we are getting down to the real reason we perform our good works, the moving force within us. So far as the deed itself is concerned, no one may know what has triggered it in the heart, but this is basic in God's evaluation. There are endless things that might motivate a Christian to perform good deeds. He may develop a sense of guilt and go out simply to do what is necessary to resolve that guilt. He may be pressured by someone who urges him to perform certain services and do what he does only because he wants to get this person off his back. He may be with a group of busy people, and he gets busy with them only because he does not want to be left out. In all these and a hundred other instances, a person may render service from a totally wrong motivation. What he does may be helpful to those he serves, yet God values his work according to his heart motivation. It is the man himself that matters with God, and without the man, the service is wood, hay or stubble.

The big question here then becomes, "What is to motivate a Christian if his service is to be accounted as gold in God's judgment?" The answer is given by Paul in 1 Corinthians. The Corinthian Christians had written to ask him some questions about spiritual gifts and their uses. He answered their questions in chapter 12 of this epistle. In the last verse of this chapter he wrote, "And moreover a most excellent way show I unto you." They had been quibbling over whether or not speaking in tongues was more important than any other spiritual gift. Paul told them that no gift is exercised rightly unless it is motivated rightly. The one thing above all else that makes any service acceptable with God is that it is motivated by love. This is clearly stated in chapter 13. It does not matter how eloquently a person may be able to speak, if his words do not issue from a heart of love, they are meaningless noise to God. A silver-voiced orator may speak the greatest truths of the gospel of Christ without being motivated by love for God and all his beautiful speaking means nothing to God.

The Christian's knowledge and faith may be extremely great, but if exercised from any motive other than love, they cease to have value to God. No giving, however sacrificial, is acceptable giving unless it stems from a heart of love. Paul distinctly said that even the giving one's body to be burned will not mean any profit unless that giving is love inspired. He urged these same Corinthians (2 Cor 9:7) to give only because their hearts moved them to give. They were not to allow someone to pressure them into giving contrary to the love of their hearts nor were they to give grudgingly. Paul did not encourage any service except that which could come from a heart of true love.

We conclude from these truths that all Christian service must spring from a heart that is moved by love if it is acceptable with God. Since this is true, it is important that we understand the meaning of the love that must motivate us in service. A great deal has been spoken and written on the meaning of four Greek words that are translated "love." It is not necessary to go into a full discussion of these four words for our purpose now; it is necessary for us to have a clear understanding of the word that is used in speaking of the love that is to motivate our hearts in service. The word Paul used is the one that is used of the highest kind of love, both divine and human. It is the love of John 3:16, thus, the love God has for men. It is the love men are to have for God as well as the love they are to have for all men. It is the word John used in saying, "God is love."

You will find varying ideas concerning the meaning of this word. I do not claim to give any meaning except what I believe is evident in the use of the word in the New Testament. This word is not used to express personal desire or liking. It contains very little, if any, sentimental value that stirs emotional feelings. Rather, there is the idea of rational and willed attitude and relationship in this word. It might be best expressed with the word "otherness." It is entirely other-centered as over against self-centered. Its main concern is for the highest good of its object, and it gladly gives itself to that end. There is no thought of "getting" in this love. Its only desire is to be able to give itself for the good of the one loved. It derives its satisfaction from knowing that its object is benefitted. This is how and why this love "never fails." It wants only to give, and when it gives, it has reached its objective.

This then, is the love that is to motivate the Christian's service. His love for God is not a feeling of an emotional sort; it is rather a deep and genuine appreciation of God that wants above all else to give itself because of love. This love for God consists of a wholehearted desire for God to be God and a willingness to be related with him in a relationship wherein he is loved and served as God. Thus my service is to be a heart response to God as my God. If I love him, I realize that I am his servant; I am happy in this relationship; and I

respond to him from my heart as I seek to express my love
with my life.

The first thing then that must characterize service, if it is
to be gold, is that it is motivated by love. Paul was accused by
some of his critics of being out of his mind because of his
commitment and enthusiastic work as Christ's servant. He
explained his attitude by writing, "For the love of Christ
constraineth us; because we thus judge, that one died for all,
therefore all died; and he died for all, that they that live
should no longer live unto themselves, but unto him who for
their sakes died and rose again" (2 Cor 5:14-15).

Even so should all Christians serve God. Christian service
must be rendered from a heart of love if it is to be rewarded.
This fact in itself rules out the possibility of rendering true
Christian service if the heart is motivated by a desire for personal gain. When God's children are moved by a heart of love
in doing what they do as his children, they then have taken
the first step toward the kind of service that is not in vain.

The second quality of true Christian service is that the
purpose of the heart must be right. At first thought we might
think there is no difference between motivation and purpose,
but we use them with a distinct difference here. The heart
motive speaks of the underlying moving cause in the heart. It
is the thing that awakens the heart to respond, the inner im-
pulse or inducement to do something; it is the heart attitude
that stimulates a person to render service, the thing that
inspires action. As we have said, this thing in true service is
love. The *purpose* refers to the outcome or results of the service. It involves a person's intention or design, his reason for
doing what he hoes, what he intends to gain through the
action.

The importance of heart purpose in Christian service is
basic in God's evaluation of that service. Jesus made this
crystal clear in his teachings. He emphasized a number of
times that a person's heart is the source of all he is and does.
Both good and evil in every life have their origin in the inner
man. Since purpose is a heart attitude, the general principle
Jesus taught applies in particular to this matter.

He discussed man's purpose in religious exercises in Matthew 6:1-18. The general truth is stated in verse 1; it is that we should be careful concerning the purpose in our hearts in all our religious activities because God's response to those works, referred to as "reward with your Father who is in heaven," depends on whether or not our purposes are what they should be. He used three kinds of religious services to illustrate: the giving of alms or money for any religious purposes, praying, and religious fasting.

The key to Jesus' teaching in all these examples is given in the words "before men to be seen of men." That is, if our service is rendered with the purpose to be seen of men, then that purpose determines the results so far as God is concerned. When a Christian gives, or prays, or fasts, with the purpose in his heart that he can through these things make an impression on his fellowmen, and when men see him and perhaps praise him for what he has done, he has received in that praise what he had in mind. This man's purpose to impress men is attained when he impresses men; therefore, this is all there is to his service so far as God is concerned; there is no further reward. On the other hand, if a person's purpose is right, and the other qualities of his service are right, then his religious works are gold in quality.

We can see that a person may have any one or more of many things in mind when he performs good works. Jesus suggested that he may do his religious "righteousnesses" to be seen of men; we suggest further that he may do things for financial gain, or he may hope to attain a selfish position. It is possible that a person may seek only personal satisfaction from the work he does and therein have a wrong purpose in his heart.

What should be a person's purpose in rendering service if it is to be acceptable with God? It is evident that our motivation and purpose are closely related; thus, when our motivation is love, our purpose would necessarily be to glorify God in all we do. To state it another way: when we are motivated by a desire to give ourselves from a heart of love, our purpose is to magnify the One we love. Since true love seeks the highest good of its object, service born of love seeks God's greatest good.

The greatest thing any human being can do for God is to glorify him. We glorify God when we relate with him and follow him as our God and do what we do in the way of service and works in an effort to induce others to do the same thing. Thus, the purpose of all we are and do should be that God may be glorified. This is precisely what Paul wrote, "Whether therefore ye eat or drink, or whatsoever ye do, do all to the glory of God (1 Cor 10:31). He wrote the same truth to the Colossians (3:17). Peter urged that every service a Christian renders should be done in order that God may be glorified (1 Pet 4:11).

This does not mean that Christian service will not be rewarded if a person has received some personal benefit from it on earth. There is always a personal blessing that comes to a faithful servant, both in the doing of the service and also in the afterglow. There are many faithful servants of God who are supported financially by the people they serve in order that they may give themselves entirely to their service. The principle we are examining here is the heart purpose of the worker. When the purpose is right, God honors the service. I believe he will richly bless this service in many ways here and now, and that the service will qualify as gold, silver, and precious stones when it comes to the final testing time.

The third quality of service that will stand the test of fire is that it must be a working God has wrought through the Christian. The matter of salvation from beginning throughout eternity is the working of God in and through individual human beings. It definitely affects what man does, but its true value lies in what God has done for man, what he actually does in man, and then in the way of Christian service, what he does through man's efforts. In other words, God must be involved in what we do if our service is to stand the test of fire.

We need to pursue this thought further. The unregenerate person is totally incapable of pleasing God for the reason that his heart is alienated from God. Since God looks on the heart and evaluates all things according to the condition of the heart, the man who is alienated in heart produces only the kind of works that come from an alienated heart. With the Christian it is totally different, because his heart has become reconciled to God and it is capable of rendering acceptable service to God. However, another factor has entered into the situation now. God's Spirit has become a vital part of the believer's life and works; his working is the actual working of God in and through the Christian. Paul said, "It is God who worketh in you both to will and to work, for his good pleasure (Phil 2:13). God moves us to work and he works through what we do.

We can see that even though this is true, yet we are still capable of doing things ourselves without God having any part in what we do. There are some things we cannot do, such as produce true spiritual results in ourselves or others. Only the Holy Spirit can bear the fruits of the Spirit. However, there are ministries to our fellowmen that we can perform, and we can do them strictly in our own wisdom and ability. As we have noted, we may do them from a selfish motive and with an unholy purpose; the whole thing can be our own doing. All service of this sort, regardless of how good it may appear to men, will be only wood, hay, and stubble when it is placed in the testing fire. We shall say more about this aspect of our service later.

Here, then, are the three qualities of service that will stand the testing by fire. The sort that will come through God's judgment fire is that which springs from a heart of love, it is rendered for the glory of God, and it is inspired and energized by the Spirit of God. According to Paul's statement, "and the fire itself will prove each man's work, of what sort it is," our works are to be tested by God's standards. As best we can discover, these are the qualities for acceptable work as set forth in the New Testament.

Paul went on to say in the passage in 1 Corinthians 3:10-15, "If any man's work shall abide which he built thereon, he shall receive a reward. If any man's works shall be burned, he shall suffer loss: but he himself shall be saved; yet so as through fire" (vv. 14-15). Thus, when our works are of the right sort, we shall be rewarded for them. This is clearly what Paul said, and we take a great deal of encouragement from the fact.

It is noteworthy that all three of the qualities we have mentioned are possible to all Christians alike. Just as faithfulness is something one person can develop as well as any other, so any person can serve God from a heart of love, for the glory of God, and he can have the Holy Spirit working in what he does. The work itself is not the determining factor. Men value things according to sensational qualities, but God values what men do on an entirely different basis. As we have noted, God places value on the heart, and in some cases, the heart attitude alone constitutes God-glorifying service.

Paul wrote about the matter of giving (2 Cor 8:12) and said that if a man has it in his heart to give and is not able to give, God looks on his heart and accepts what he would have done had he been able. So we can know for sure that God will determine the matter of rewards fairly; there will be no mistakes or slip-ups when our works are tried by fire. The gold, silver, and precious stone service will come through purified and will be rewarded; the wood, hay, and stubble will vanish into ashes and the worker will suffer loss-he will receive no reward for what he did on earth.

We come then to answer the question that heads this section, "Will all good works be rewarded?" The answer is that rewards for "good works" depend on whether or not the works are truly good as God determines goodness. If our works are good, that is, if they measure up to these three qualities we have noted, they will be rewarded. On the other hand, if the service we render is selfishly done, it must be classified as wood, hay, or stubble; it will not be the basis for rewards. Paul said that the person who renders this kind of service will suffer loss, yet he himself will be saved. He will retain the eternal life that God has given him; he will continue the kind of spiritual person he has become, but he will not receive a reward for the wood, hay, or stubble kind of work he did.

What Will Rewards Be?

*Y*ou may say, "Well, it's about time!" We have seemingly been going in circles, looking at this matter from first one viewpoint, then from another. Finally, we come to look directly at rewards in heaven in an effort to discover just what they will be. Let us be perfectly honest in giving an answer; anything we shall say must be understood as a personal opinion.

So far as I know, there is no forthright description of rewards for Christian service. Jesus said that under certain conditions, they would be *great* (Matt 5:12). He also said they would be of "your Father" (Matt 6:1). Jesus also referred to "a prophet's reward" and to "a righteous man's reward" (Matt 10:41). Paul said that every man would receive his *own* reward (1 Cor 3:8), and John mentioned a *full* reward (2 John 8). Beyond terms like these we are not told what rewards will be, therefore, we must formulate our personal opinions if we seek to answer our question.

This is just what I propose to do; I ask that you consider these suggestions as personal opinion rather than any claim that I have the last word on the subject. I do believe that these opinions are in harmony with scriptural principles and I have derived a great deal of personal satisfaction from considering them. I have not been able to find any written material whatsoever on this particular aspect of our subject other than the scriptural principles that will be mentioned. I recommend these ideas wholeheartedly and trust that you will be able to understand them clearly.

Earlier in our study we mentioned the idea that differences in spiritual maturity might be illustrated by referring to different size containers. Each may be full, but one holds more than the other. Some people will simply be able to enjoy heaven more than others. While I believe this is true concerning spiritual maturity, I do not consider spiritual maturity and rewards for service the same thing. Rewards will be something different from capacity to enjoy heaven.

We have also taken note of the claim that all ideas of reward for Christian service are unchristian and we said at that time we would explain the meaning of rewards later so as to dispel that claim. We have come to that time. Just what will rewards in heaven consist of? What will they mean to the person who is rewarded?

When we speak of a reward for something we have done in this life, we usually think of it as something given to us for our own personal benefit and enjoyment. A reward is thought of as something that enhances our life; its value lies chiefly in what we derive from it. Because of this understanding of the meaning of rewards, it seems unchristian to serve God with rewards in mind. However, the New Testament repeatedly urges us to serve God faithfully with the assurance that we shall be rewarded, so we conclude that the commonly understood meaning of rewards in this life is not applicable to heavenly rewards.

Rewards as taught in the New Testament must have a meaning that is in harmony with the qualities of service we have noted. It is evident that we can serve God rightly and in doing so, realize that God will reward us for that service. The explanation of this harmonious relation between right service and an eye for rewards lies in the meaning of heavenly rewards.

We find our solution in a consideration of heaven's table of values; just what is truly worthwhile in God's evaluation of things? Is it not clear that God does not see things as we see them in this world? Remember, Isaiah insisted that God's ways are higher than our ways and his thoughts differ from our thoughts. This truth applies in regard to the meaning of rewards. God has revealed that we shall be rewarded for the right kind of service. He means one thing while most of us have thought he meant something else. A reward from God's viewpoint is something that is truly for our good. He places no value on what ordinary men want, such as worldly fame, profit, or pleasure.

Jesus said that the servant who is faithful in his work will be counted a blessed person when his master comes (Luke 12:43). The blessedness will be due to the fact that he will be rewarded, "He will set him over all he hath." The blessedness and the reward are the same thing; we shall know something of the meaning of rewards if we can discover the meaning of blessedness as Jesus used it.

Jesus used this word quite often in speaking of the status or condition of certain Christians. It is difficult to express the meaning of the word when applied to Christians in the world; it is more difficult to understand its meaning when applied to God's children in heaven.

You will recognize right away that this is the word repeated in each of the Beatitudes in the Sermon on the Mount (Matt 5:3-12). Some translators use the word "happy" to express the meaning, which is perhaps the best English word we have to carry the meaning of the original. However, we must define the meaning of "happy" or we shall miss the deeper meaning intended in the word.

We have already noted some things about the meaning of the word, so let us review what we said earlier. We often use the word "happy" in speaking of shallow emotional reaction to our immediate surroundings. When circumstances are pleasant, we are happy, but when circumstances change, happiness disappears. Thus, this kind of happiness is dictated by "happenstance." It is very unstable and is subject to sudden change to unhappiness of a similar order.

The blessedness Jesus spoke of is something far different from this shallow response to surface events in life. The happiness Jesus spoke of is the kind that can result from mourning for sins, or is present during persecution, so it could not mean a feeling of pleasantness that grows out of favorable circumstances. The happiness Jesus spoke of refers to a quality of being that characterizes a person. In this life true blessedness consists of a realization of a right, settled, and permanent relationship with God, along with the assurance that all of life's concerns can safely be left to his care. Jesus assured his apostles just before his crucifixion that although they would be filled with sorrow because of what was about to happen, later they would see him again and they would be filled with a joy that no person or condition could take from them (John 16:22).

Blessedness in this life is true peace of heart that is derived from God's forgiving grace; it is a sense of well-being because one is in Jesus Christ. This happiness is not dependent on any physical or material circumstance, for it has its source in God. The things that increase this blessedness are those things that contribute to our true relationship with God, or that help us to understand the relationship we have so as to rest in it more confidently. This is the substance of Jesus' teaching in the Beatitudes, as well as in all the other uses of the term "blessed" when applied to his children in this life.

The meaning of blessedness in heaven must be considered similar to true blessedness on earth, only it will be of a fuller and deeper quality. All of God's children will be blessed in heaven, as we noted earlier, but Jesus indicates that rewards for service will mean a greater blessing in some way. Just exactly what this difference will be we cannot say, but it is evident from Jesus' statement that there will be a difference. The difference will not be something that the individual can consider as a selfish possession to be kept to himself. Perhaps a further word will help to clarify the matter.

We often speak of natural law in referring to the way our world functions. Scientists have been able to discover many principles according to which things in our material universe operate. We feel sure there are others yet to be discovered. We rely on these principles in every area of our physical existence and think nothing of accepting them as final. When we ignore some particular principle, we expect to suffer the consequences, that is, we do if we are mature enough to exercise common sense.

The Bible reveals that there are also certain spiritual and moral principles that apply to us in this area that are equally reliable. These principles are clearly stated in the Bible and example after example is given in the lives of the people whose experiences are recorded there. Some of these principles have to do with cause and effect. An example of this is Paul's statement of the principle that applies to sowing and reaping (Gal 6:7-8). The principle that can help us at this point deals more with those things that determine the meaning and value of personhood. There are certain things that yield one kind of person and others that produce a totally different kind of person. Or, to apply the principle to our present matter, there are certain things that result in greater happiness than others. When Jesus said that the faithful servant would be especially blessed because of that faithfulness, he meant that he would receive that which would yield true happiness.

We must put out of our minds our earthly table of values and try to understand the truth Jesus spoke. When we do, we shall realize that true blessedness does not depend upon what we get as an end in itself. The big lie and cheat of this world is the belief that our happiness depends on our having what we want and being rid of what we do not like. Jesus said there is greater blessedness is what we give than in what we get (Acts 20:35). The happiness that comes to us from what we get in shallow and fleeting.

Real and lasting happiness results from the giving of ourselves to the glory of God and the good of our fellowman. We do not give in order to be blessed; that would not be true giving. We give because we love and want to benefit the one we love. The very spirit of true giving is forgetting any getting and thinking only of the giving. It is the principle of the seed falling into the ground and dying; only in this manner can it live and produce. Even so, only as a human being gives himself and his service is there true blessedness to be received.

We need to recognize this principle and then to understand the meaning of rewards for Christian service in the light of it. What will rewards in heaven be? They will consists of *greater abilities, more opportunities,* and *greater efficiency* in rendering service to the glory of God. They will not be something that is given to the individual to have for his own personal benefit, but something that will enable him to give himself in a fuller sense. Since it is true that it is more blessed to give than to receive, this kind of reward will bring true riches to the person. However, we must keep in mind that this will have no tinge of selfish indulgence in it. We must know that God is supremely happy in the deepest meaning of that word. He is happy because he is perfect love. The happiness of our rewards will be of a similar nature to God's own blessedness. Thus Jesus said the faithful servant would be blessed when his Master comes because he would be given greater areas in which to exercise himself as a faithful servant.

This idea is foreign to our earthly minds, for we think of being rewarded for faithful service by being relieved of further serving. We look forward to the great leap at the age of sixty-five, because then we will have earned retirement. We think of retirement as the time when we shall no longer have the responsibilities of hewing to the line in working hours and production results. We are rewarded for faithful work by taking a vacation for the rest of our lives. Because of this prevailing idea, we find it difficult to think of being rewarded by being given greater abilities and increased opportunities, even though it be with added enablement.

One of the blessed facts about life in heaven is that we shall be free from these self-centered, worldly distortions of truth. Even now, when we give it serious thought, we realize the true blessedness in this idea. Really, God could not reward us in a richer way than by endowing us with greater abilities, opening up vaster fields of service, and in it all, supplying unlimited power to do the job perfectly. In heaven we will have become totally centered upon the glory of God. We shall neither desire nor seek anything else. The joy bells of our souls will be set to ringing as we are used to magnify him. To know that we are used of him, to be pleasing in his sight, to pour ourselves out in some way on his behalf, will be the constant desire of our hearts and will bring the deepest blessedness that is possible. Heavenly bliss will consist in losing selfish inclination and coming to be fully God-centered. This will characterize all of God's children, but the ability to serve him in a greater way will be determined by our rewards for earthly faithfulness in service.

We know that even now with all the carnal interferences we have, we derive our most satisfying joys from *giving* ourselves to bless others. We can surely see that there could not be a richer meaning of rewards in heaven for us. The child of God who has been given some ability to use for God's glory and man's good on earth, and who has been faithful in the use of the talent, could not want anything better than to be enabled to use that gift in a greater way for eternity.

We do not know exactly what service in heaven will be. The one thing that will matter is that we shall serve God. John was told in his vision (Rev 7:15) that those before the throne of God served him day and night in the Temple of God. The picture John was given is one of perfection in the field of service. God's servants are to be protected, provided for, and are to serve under the great Shepherd of their souls; there will be no cause or occasion for tears; thus, their service will be one continuous relationship of joy and blessedness.

We realize that serving God on earth is a matter of serving men. We love, worship, and praise God in various ways, but we serve God as we minister to men. Jesus said that visiting and ministering to the needy is the same as rendering the service to him (Matt 25:40). Since there will be no physical needs in heaven, we wonder just what service will be. We are not given an answer to this question, so we must leave it without an answer. We might suggest that a person who has been endowed with a beautiful voice on earth and has developed and used it for the glory of God during his lifetime, could be rewarded with an even more beautiful voice and given the opportunity to sing God's praises in heaven.

Whatever the particular aspects of service may be, we may rest assured that all of it will be done in a manner that is in harmony with God and that the rendering of that service will be reward enough to fill the heart with joy. Each individual will be rewarded *according* to his service. The rewards we receive will determine the degree of our blessedness. This much we are convinced is revealed in the Bible; further details must await our own personal realization in that day when

God shall render to every man according to what he has done, whether it be good or bad.

Let us summarize what we have said about the Christian's existence in heaven. We have stated that three things will determine our status there. First, we shall be children of God who are spiritually alive with the life of God. This will be true of all who are in heaven. Second, we have said that we shall be the same spiritual person in heaven we have become on earth. In this area, we shall not be alike; there will be differences just as there are differences now. Third, we shall be rewarded according to our service. Our rewards will make a difference in our blessedness in heaven. Our understanding of the meaning of these ideas is limited now. We have noted that John says it has not been revealed fully what we shall be; thus we accept what has been revealed and, rejoicing in that, leave the remainder in God's hand, knowing by faith it will be according to everything we have experienced with God in this life.

And just what have we learned from experience with God? Suppose we answer this question with a brief discussion of a term Paul used in speaking of our Christian experience with the Holy Spirit. He referred to the *earnest* of the spirit as God's gift to us (2 Cor 1:22; 5:5; Eph 1:14). This word "earnest" is used primarily in speaking of money given as a pledge on a contract, assuring the full payment later. It also expresses the idea of foretaste, as suggested in Hebrews 6:5. This aspect of our experience is also expressed in the word "first-fruits" of the Spirit (Rom 8:23). Paul wrote that even though we have the firstfruits, we still long for the full redemption that will be ours in the resurrection. The firstfruits of the Holy Spirit consist of our experiences in this life in which we partake of the Holy Spirit and have true spiritual fellowship with God. This truth was expressed by Paul in the use of the word that is translated "the heavenlies." He said that God has blessed us in Christ with spiritual blessings "in the heavenlies" (Eph 1:3). He also said that God made us to sit with Christ "in the heavenlies" (Eph 2:6).

All three of these terms, the earnest of the Spirit, the first-fruits of the Spirit, and the heavenlies, speak of our direct, personal, spiritual experiences with God in the Person of the Holy Spirit. This taste of God is the real thing; it is a foretaste of heaven itself. Our highest spiritual experiences on earth tell us that this is what heaven will be. The Holy Spirit in us is truly the essence of heaven in us now. The difference between now and eternity is a matter of degree, for here "we see through a glass darkly" and here we experience the Holy Spirit in our limited physical bodies, but in heaven we shall see, know, and experience God directly and without the hindrances we now have.

All of this adds up to a grand and glorious eternity that can be described only as heavenly. The more we study and think about it, and especially the more we try to express our thoughts, the more limited we feel in our ability to do so. It is hard to talk about heaven in a satisfactory way. We thank God for what we know, and we thank him for what we believe, even though we cannot understand some of it.

Now, about That Title

*A*ll this time we have been talking about the conditions we believe will prevail in heaven. Our primary concern has been what heaven will be and mean to us; we have not even hinted at an answer to the title of this book, so it's about time we turn our attention to this matter. This means we must think about heaven itself, its nature and where it is. These two things pretty well outline this section for us. We shall think first of the nature of heaven, what kind of place it is. Then we shall consider where heaven is.

Just what kind of place is heaven anyway? Heaven is a spiritual place; it is characterized by spiritual life, and is the eternal abiding place of God. Heaven does not consist of material substances in any way, nor is it dependent on them. To realize this we need only to recall that before God spoke this universe of material things into existence, he was in his eternal home that we call heaven. Heaven existed before material substances were created, thus it is not dependent upon them in any fashion nor does it consist of them to any degree. Heaven is a spiritual reality that has always existed, separate and apart from the material things we know in our material universe.

We must be careful in our thinking not to limit reality to material substances. This material universe is real, but it is not the only reality in existence. Nonmaterial realities exist just as truly as do the material. Our minds are prone to think of reality only in terms of physical and material substances and to reject as imaginary or unreal anything that is purely spiritual. The naturalistic mind of the unregenerate person may well deny the reality of spiritual things, for as Paul noted, "the natural mind receiveth not the things of the Spirit of God." However, this is not true of the child of God; he should not limit reality to things he can experience with one of his five physical senses. If anyone accepts the spiritual as real, a person who has been born again should be that person.

However, even the Christian sometimes finds it difficult to accept anything as real unless it is physical and material. This is partly because we live in a material world and partly because any reference to nonmaterial things must be stated in words that carry earthly ideas.

For instance, there are a number of statements about God that attribute physical qualities to him. He is said to sit, to come and go, to look down upon earth, to have eyes and a right hand, to hear, and to perform many other similar actions that are physical. We speak of these terms as "anthropomorphisms"; that is, terms that apply human qualities and actions to God. We are not to interpret these words as teaching that God has a physical body. We are clearly told that "God is Spirit," so we know that he does not have a physical body.

In speaking of what God does, we must use human terms for the simple reason that we have no other vocabulary with which to describe God and his actions. When the Bible says that Jesus sat down on the right hand of the Father (Heb 10:12), we are to understand the symbolic meaning of the right hand. Jesus is in the place of highest honor and power, second only to the Father. In our human relationships, the position at a ruler's right hand always carries this meaning, and this is the meaning of such terms when applied to God. We are not to think of God as having a physical body like ours. We were created in God's image, but this does not refer to a physical body. We are like God in being a person with the qualities of personhood and with the possibility of becoming a child of God spiritually.

We must recognize a similar difficulty in the words used in the Bible in its descriptions of heaven. We read of the streets of gold, of pearly gates, of rivers of water, of a tree of life, of our many mansions, and many other terms that might lead us to believe that heaven consists of physical and material substances.

Some of us insist that we must take the Bible literally and conclude that the streets of heaven will be paved with real gold just like we have on earth. Somehow we overlook the fact that the Bible also teaches that the material universe is temporal rather than eternal. Peter referred to the fact that gold will come through a fire purified, yet it will eventually perish (1 Pet 1:7). He also assured us that the time will come when the elements will be dissolved and the earth will be consumed by fire (2 Pet 3:10). We must conclude that since heaven is eternal, it is spiritual, not material.

The descriptions of heaven in the Bible assure us that it is a place of unparalleled beauty and unequaled splendor. Words of material substances are used because we do not have any other words to describe spiritual reality. We are to understand that what "streets of gold" means to us in this world, heaven is from a spiritual viewpoint.

We are not to conclude from these observations that heaven is only a state or condition of existence. It is more than a subjective or inner attitude of mind and heart. The Bible pictures heaven as a real place where God is, where Jesus went when he died, where the redeemed are, and where all of God's children go at death. What we are saying is that it is a spiritual place and that material substances cannot possibly be a part of it. Paul said that flesh and blood, or the physical body, cannot inherit God's kingdom (1 Cor 15:50). The substance of his argument in this passage is that since this is true, when Christ returns to receive his children into heaven, those who are alive must be transformed before he can receive them. They cannot go into heaven in physical bodies because heaven is a spiritual place of a totally different nature from this world.

The Christian is born into God's kingdom spiritually when he is saved, but before he can enter into heaven, he must either die and leave this body, or he must be transformed when Christ returns to earth. In this life the physical and spiritual are bound together in us, but either physical death or the transformation must free the spirit from the body before it can go to heaven. The material elements that make up our physical bodies must remain in this material universe for the simple reason that there is no other place they can exist.

The second thing we suggested is the location of heaven. Where on earth is heaven? Let me hasten to correct a possible implication in the question. We might get the impression that heaven is located someplace on earth, and this question seeks to pinpoint that place. This is not what the question is intended to suggest; the "on earth" phrase is not intended to suggest that heaven is on earth at all. In fact, the key truth of this book is the belief and claim that heaven as a spiritual place transcends space. Heaven does not consist of material substances nor is it localized in some place in this material universe. Heaven is eternal and thus transcends time; it is also spiritual and transcends space.

We often think and speak of heaven as "up there," or "out there" some where in space. Perhaps we have never stopped to try to determine just exactly where, but we have a feeling that somewhere out there in space, at some particular spot, heaven must be located. The truth is that heaven is "up there" only in the sense that it is a higher kind of place as to quality; space does not even enter into the difference at all. There is no one place in the universe where a person is nearer heaven than he is any other place. It is difficult for our space-oriented minds to comprehend the idea, but we would be as near heaven a billion light-years out in space as we are on earth. When we say that heaven transcends space, we mean that it is neither confined in, nor excluded from space anywhere or to any degree. Heaven is a totally different kind of place from this material universe.

This means that the material universe and heaven are both real and that they exist together without either one necessarily affecting or being affected by the other. Perhaps an illustration will clarify the idea. In our day of electronic communications we are aware of the existence of what we call ether waves. We realize that in certain places within the range of a broadcasting station we are encompassed with the sounds transmitted from that station. We cannot hear them with our natural ear. The same thing is true of the television pictures; they surround us, yet we cannot see those pictures with our physical eyes unless we have a receiving set that can convert the electronic impulses into visible pictures. The sounds and pictures are all around us when we are in the area of the broadcasting station, yet we may not affect them nor do they affect us until we are made aware of them, provide the sets necessary for reception, and tune in to make the communication complete.

In a very similar way, heaven as a spiritual reality is as truly one place as it is any other. The electronic impulses from a radio broadcasting station must go from the station to the receiving set, thus they are related to the ether waves, or this material universe. Heaven as a spiritual reality is not dependent upon any physical or material conveyor; it is spiritual and exists in and of itself as spiritual. At the same time, the similarity stands in the illustration. Heaven is as truly "here" as the radio sounds are here. Furthermore, the same heaven is as truly everywhere as it is here. Neither space nor time is involved in the reality of heaven; it both transcends and permeates space.

We have already suggested that heaven existed before material elements were created, therefore it is distinct from and does not consist of material substances. Now let us project ourselves through imagination into the presence of God before this material universe was created. He was in heaven and heaven was where? It was exactly where it had been from eternity; it is still "where" it has always been. Today, it is a realm of spiritual reality coexisting with this material universe. Someone has suggested that heaven is another dimension, a spiritual dimension. Perhaps this is as good a term as we can find. It is a spiritual realm or dimension characterized by spiritual life, and is as much right here as it is anywhere. If we had the capacity, we could "see" heaven just as truly as we see things in this world with our physical eyes. The fact is that heaven is as near us as the radio ether waves are. God is definitely not "out there" somewhere in space. There is a thin line between these two realms of existence for the Christian; it is a line that is not remotely related with space. It is totally a spiritual matter.

When we are made alive to God, God himself in the Person of the Holy Spirit enters into our spirit and indwells us. The Spirit of God becomes his direct communication with our spirit; thus in a real way, we have a relationship with heaven. We worship God in the Spirit, so there is a bit of heaven in a true worship service. When we pray, we do not broadcast a message to some far-off place in the universe. Prayer is fellowship with God through the Holy Spirit; we need only to tune our spirit to his Spirit, and the communication is made. The time or place does not matter; Jesus assured the Samaritan woman of this fact (John 4:21-24). Some of our astronauts knew God's presence on the moon just as truly as they had known it on earth, for space has nothing to do with spiritual reality.

We have a way of talking about going to heaven when we die as though somehow we intend to take a long journey to some faraway paradise in the skies. We do not seem to know just where it is or how we shall get there, but we think in terms of going to some place in space. Really, physical death only sets our spirit free from its imprisonment in our physical body and this material universe and allows it to be transferred into heaven. When the Christian dies, his spirit is not carried through the trackless wastes of space to some remote resting place called heaven. The moment he is released from this body he is across the "line" and awakens in the presence of God in heaven, for heaven is actually that near. Paul told the men at Athens that God is not far from each one of us, for "in him we live, and move, and have our being" (Acts 17:27-28).

This belief concerning the nature of heaven explains many of the events recorded in the Bible that are otherwise difficult to understand. All the experiences men have had with God as recorded in the Bible take on new meaning when we interpret them in the light of the idea that heaven is not located in some far-off spot in the universe. All of God's communications with men are best understood when we realize that space in no way affects his contact with this world. Someone has noted that the Old Testament prophets claimed God's communication with them some twenty-four hundred times in words like these: "The word of the Lord came unto me." Likely, much of this was subjective communication, but there were times when men heard the voice of God speaking. In such cases, it seems clear that God did not need to broadcast his message by means of the ether waves; he simply made his speaking audible to the particular man to whom he was speaking. Distance had nothing whatsoever to do with his communication.

The appearances of angels to men in biblical accounts did not necessitate a jet trip through space for the angels; they were simply enabled to make themselves visible to men, to speak so as to be heard, and thus to communicate their messages. Again, space is no barrier to angels anymore than it is to God.

Another example of this principle is given in the experience of Elisha and his servant. They were surrounded by their enemies, the Syrians, and the servant of Elisha was terrified because of their plight; but when the prophet of God prayed, the young man's eyes were opened to see that they were also surrounded by the hosts of heaven, and the young man's fears disappeared. God enabled this young man to see what had been there all along.

We find a similar example in the experience of Stephen at the time he was stoned to death. We are told in the account in the book of Acts that he, "being full of the Holy Spirit, looked up steadfastly into heaven, and saw the glory of God, and Jesus standing on the right hand of God." In the theory of heaven which is being presented, this means that Stephen was simply enabled to penetrate the "veil of separation" between the material and the spiritual and to see the Son of man standing on the right hand of God. This type of experience is referred to as a vision, but there is more in it than a mental image flashed upon the screen of the mind when a man like Stephen is endowed with the ability to get a glimpse of heaven. Likely, in a technical sense, Stephen's eyes did not see into heaven, for the purely physical is not capable of seeing the purely spiritual; for all practical purposes, however, it was equal to the same thing. We might rightly conclude that so far as relation and possibility are concerned, any spiritually alive person could be enabled to see into heaven at any time. Heaven is just that *close.*

The experiences of Jesus Christ may be understood more clearly through this understanding of heaven as a spiritual place coexisting with our material world. In the transfiguration of Jesus, the glory of the spiritual greatly affected even the physical body of Jesus. The voice of the Father became audible to the three apostles who were present.

Again, after his resurrection, Jesus was able to appear and to disappear at will. Although we may speak of his *coming and going,* it was not a matter of spatial traveling; it was rather an appearing and disappearing as these affected men in space. Many have questioned how he got into the upper room where the disciples were meeting, taking for granted that the doors were locked. This theory of heaven renders all such questioning unnecessary. Jesus simply appeared in this realm of space and enabled men to see him.

We could consider all of the experiences of men with God that are recorded in the Bible and find that they take on new meaning when viewed through this concept of heaven as a spiritual place coexisting with our universe.

This theory of heaven is the only way my mind can conceive of the omnipresence of God in a satisfactory manner. How can God be everywhere at the same time? From a purely materialistic viewpoint, he could not be at more than one place in space at any given time. However, if heaven is a spiritual place that is not limited by space or time, then he is as truly present everywhere as he is anywhere. That is, God is not limited to space, yet he is immanent in space.

The question might be raised as to what the "new heaven and new earth" of which the Bible speaks will be. There is no clear answer to this question in the Bible so far as I can discover, so we are left to personal opinion on the subject. Whether God will create something altogether new and different from the present heaven, only he knows. The old things, the things we now know as the material universe, will pass away according to Peter, "But the day of the Lord will come as a thief; in the which the heavens shall pass away with a great noise, and the elements shall be dissolved with fervent heat, and the earth and the works that are therein shall be burned up" (2 Pet 3:10). He went on to say in verse 13 of the same chapter: "But, according to his promise, we look for new heavens and a new earth, wherein dwelleth righteousness." The nature of this newness is not explained in the Bible, so we must refrain from trying to be exact in our description of the new heaven and new earth.

We must be content while we live in this world with limited understanding of heaven, knowing by faith that whereas "now we see in a mirror darkly," one day we shall see "face to face." We understand that now "we know in part" only, but one day, "when that which is perfect is come, that which is in part shall be done away," and we shall "know fully even as also" we have been fully known. Heaven in every way will be far greater than the best we have known on earth, for earth has no gold that is as precious and glorious as the gold that will pave the streets of heaven. Earth has no light as brilliant as the light of the Son of God that will illumine heaven. Earth has no jewels as resplendent as the gates of pearls that swing in heaven. One day we shall sing with fullness of meaning:

> Fade, fade, each earthly joy;
> Jesus is mine.
> Break every tender tie;
> Jesus is mine. . . .
>
> Perishing things of clay,
> Born but for one brief day,
> Pass from my heart away;
> Jesus is mine!
>
> *Theodore E. Perkins*

From Earth to Heaven

*A*s we fill our minds with these wonderful thoughts concerning our eternal home in heaven, we find our hearts aglow with hope and aspiration. We rejoice with Paul (1 Cor 15:54) in knowing that one day death is to be "swallowed up" and eternal life will reign forever. The final triumph of Jesus Christ over sin will be over death itself (1 Cor 15:26). We can hardly think of our total victory in Christ without rejoicing in the final destruction of man's greatest enemy in this life, which is death.

When our thoughts are carried to this great height of triumph, however, we are constantly reminded with Paul (1 Cor 15:55) that we are still in the flesh and that until Christ does return, we shall eventually be at the mercy of physical death. One day, death will be no more; but until that great day, death is a reality every human being must reckon with. For most people, death is perhaps the starkest reality of all things in this life. We as physical human beings have a natural desire to live and our minds feel a revulsion against what death does to the things we love so dearly in this life. Our scientists have searched diligently for methods and means of prolonging physical life on earth and have accomplished marvelous things in regard to warding off death temporarily. Yet we know all too well that regardless of all we or others may do, if Jesus delays his return, we shall die. From the moment of man's first sin, death has been doing its work in every mortal creature. The psalmist marveled that all men eventually die. The writer of Ecclesiastes (2:15-16) bemoaned the fact that neither wisdom nor riches was respected by death, "As it happeneth to the fool, so will it happen even to me," he wailed, and went on to express his disappointment further, "And how doth the wise man die even as the fool!"

Our purpose in this section of our study is to investigate the questions involved in our transfer from this material universe into the spiritual realm of heaven. Let us frankly admit

that many questions do flood our minds as we stand before
a casket and look upon the dead body lying in it.

"Where is he now?"

"Is he conscious and in the presence of God?"

"Is it really true that a Christian who has died is happier
in heaven than he was on earth?"

"Do we go directly to heaven when we die, or is there an
intermediate place where we must await the resurrection?"

As we seek answers to these questionings of our probing
minds, we need to keep several things before us. One, we are
delving into an area of existence that is beyond scientific
methods of research. There are no natural means by which
man can investigate the realm of spiritual reality. The greatest
scientific mind in existence is on the same level with the sim-
plest mind: both must rely on divine revelation for truth
concerning these matters. Men have gone to the moon and
have returned with evidence to substantiate their findings.

We have not discovered any way by which man can ex-
plore the realms of heaven, experience the conditions there,
and return to earth with evidence to prove his findings. However, God has come to earth in the Person of his Son; he died
and rose again to assure us of life beyond death. He is now
dwelling on earth in the spirits of his redeemed children, and
he has revealed through the Bible a great deal about life after
death. This is the source of our search for answers to our questions concerning life after death. What we find in the Bible
should be carefully examined with an open mind and
accepted by faith as God's truth. God has not revealed all the
details our searching minds would like to know, so we must
understand what he has revealed and leave the unrevealed to
him, knowing that he is to be trusted in all things. We can rest
assured that he has revealed all we truly need to know, so
that is what we seek now.

Perhaps the first thing we would like to have settled is the
matter as to whether we continue a conscious existence after
death, or is there a period of unconscious existence between
physical death and the resurrection. This was the import of
Job's question, "If a man die, does he go on living?" This is

our thought in the presence of death, "Is this person alive and conscious somewhere?" Death seems to be so total and final, and so far as the physical body is concerned, it is both. But what about the spirit of the person? Has it entered into a state of unconsciousness or is the person as truly alive and conscious as he has ever been?

Logic seems to say that one of four things is possible for a human soul at physical death. First, he could simply cease to exist in any sense of the meaning of existence. This is the contention of the person who rejects the existence of God and of life after death; nothing exists beyond this life on earth. Second, one's spirit or soul may enter into an unconscious existence that many call soul sleep. This belief holds that there is no awareness of existence between physical death and the resurrection on the part of the individual. Third, there may be an intermediate place between earth and heaven where souls remain during the period between physical death and the resurrection. Fourth, the soul of man enters directly into either heaven or hell at death in a conscious condition. Let us look at each of these ideas in the light of the teachings of the Bible.

The first idea that physical death is the end of existence for a human being is a purely naturalistic view. I remember reading an article in a daily newspaper years ago written by a natural scientist who said that so far as we can ascertain from science, there is nothing beyond physical death. There is no questioning of this opinion; there is no scientific evidence of the existence of spiritual reality. The reason is that material substances and spiritual reality are entirely different kinds of existences. Spiritual subsistence is not subject to material confirmation, thus it is only natural that life beyond death cannot be substantiated by means of scientific research. If we rely solely on empirical proof, that is, evidence that can be experienced by one of our five physical senses, we are left without any reliable evidence that the human soul continues to exist after physical death.

When we accept divine revelation, however, we find a totally different situation. The Bible begins its account of the existence of this material universe by assuming that God and spiritual reality are eternal; only this material universe had a beginning. Throughout the biblical revelation, the material universe is considered temporal while spiritual reality is presented as only temporarily confined to this body and truly eternal in nature. The dominant note of the New Testament is eternal life through Jesus Christ; remove this note and life on earth becomes meaningless while death remains as man's greatest enemy. The Christian does not look to natural science for evidence of continuing life after death; his hope is built on faith in God's revelation of truth.

The second theory must be examined more fully, for it has gained quite a following and those who propagate the idea claim scriptural justification for their teachings. The claim is that when one dies, his soul enters into a state of unconscious sleep and remains in the grave until the return of Christ, when the soul will be awakened and the body will be raised.

This belief is derived from metaphorical statements in the Bible that are interpreted in a physical sense. In the Old Testament, physical death is most often referred to as sleep. Such statements as, "Thou shalt sleep with thy fathers" (Deut 31:16), are the common way in which the writers referred to physical death.

Similar statements are used in the New Testament, such as "for the damsel is not dead, but sleepeth" (Matt 9:24); "many bodies of the saints that had fallen asleep were raised" (Matt 27:52); "These things spake he; and after this he saith unto them, Our friend Lazarus is fallen asleep; but I go that I may awake him out of sleep" (John 11:11). This reference to death as sleep is to be interpreted as metaphorical language; it is not intended to be understood as teaching an unconscious state of the person, but is used of the physical body.

The word for "sleep" literally means "to lie down"; this would not be used of the person or soul of men; it is plainly a term applicable only to the physical body.

This kind of language was used for two reasons. First, the body in death appears to be asleep, and this terminology would be a natural way to express the state of the body. Second, then as now, we tend to use language in speaking of stark realities that will soften the impact of those realities. As a rule, we do not say that a person has died; we usually prefer to say that he has passed away, or he has departed this life, or he has gone to his reward. We choose some wording that avoids the harshness of the word death.

The claim is also made that none of those who were raised from the dead gave any indication they were conscious during the time they were dead. This is only as we would expect it to be. When people were raised from the dead, they came back to life on earth with no memory of what occurred during the time they were dead. God intends that all men live on earth in a "faith relationship" with him. He does not prove himself by physical means for he wants all men to accept his word. Thus, these people who were raised from the dead could not be allowed to retain their memory of what life after death was. Paul testified that he had a vision in which he saw things that were unlawful to speak (2 Cor 12:4).

A further argument is that statements are made in the Bible that the dead are unconscious. The psalmist wrote, "For in death there is no remembrance of thee: In Sheol, who shall give thee thanks?" (Ps 6:5). In all statements of this kind, the meaning again applies only to the physical. So far as the kind of praise men ascribe to God in the physical body on earth is concerned, there is none beyond physical death. The tongue is silenced in death; the human mind ceases to function; but, the spirit of man is not included in these statements. That this is true will be shown shortly when we consider positive teachings in the New Testament.

In addition to these claims, it is contended that the teaching of a judgment for all men is contrary to the belief that men go directly either to heaven or to hell. It is said that there would be no purpose for the judgment if men had already been in heaven or hell. This claim is made because of a misunderstanding of the purpose of the judgment. We shall discuss this purpose later, but for now simply say that eternal destiny is settled before the judgment. There is nothing inconsistent with the dead going immediately to heaven or hell at

death and then coming before the judgment, when we understand the nature and purpose of the judgment.

We should base our beliefs concerning this subject on
plain direct statements from the New Testament instead of
selecting passages that merely allow for interpretations that fit
into our theories. Many false ideas are held because we fail to
realize that the truth concerning life and immortality was not
revealed until Jesus Christ came. This means that God did not
reveal to Old Testament saints the full truth about life beyond
physical death. They were given faint glimmerings of truth
sufficient for a belief in life after death, but they were not
given particular details. Paul wrote that life and immortality
were brought to light through the gospel (2 Tim 1:9-10).

Beyond the fact of existence after death, nothing about
that existence is made clear in the Old Testament. The rabbis
developed elaborate theories concerning the state of the dead,
but these theories are not substantiated in the Old Testament.

The word *sheol* is used in the Old Testament in speaking
of life after death. This word means simply the abode of the
dead; it does not contain any particular details of that existence, thus we can conclude from this word only that there is
an abode of the dead. Beyond this fact the Old Testament
does not go; the people may have had different concepts, but
we cannot accept either rabbinic teaching or the common
understanding of the people as a basis for the truth. We must
not formulate our belief on this matter from surmisings drawn
from Old Testament statements. Eternal life and the status of
the dead are subjects that were not revealed by God until
Jesus Christ came, taught, lived, died, and rose again from the
dead. Thus, we must look to the New Testament for our
knowledge on these matters.

What then do we find in the New Testament concerning
a continuing conscious existence of the soul beyond death?
First, let us consider some teachings of Jesus Christ. In his discussion with the Sadducees on this subject (Matt 22:23-33),
Jesus quoted Exodus 3:6, ". . . I am the God of Abraham, the
God of Isaac, and the God of Jacob? God is not the God of the
dead, but of the living." This clearly indicates that Abraham,

Isaac, and Jacob were alive; they were not asleep in their graves. In harmony with this statement we find that when Jesus was transfigured, Moses and Elijah came to talk with him. Again, we must conclude that they were alive and conscious, not asleep in their graves.

While Jesus was on the cross, one of the thieves asked him to remember him when he came into his kingdom. Jesus said to him, "Today shalt thou be with me in Paradise." The word "Paradise" means "the Garden of God," that is, the place where God is. Any idea other than this is reading meaning into the word it did not have at the time of its use. In other words, Paradise was another term used in speaking of heaven. The theory that this word indicates some place between death and heaven is based upon rabbinic theories of life after death; it is not according to the teachings of the New Testament. When Jesus died, he said to his Father, "Father, into they hands I commit my spirit." Unless we have some theory to defend, this statement can mean only that when Jesus died, he went immediately and directly into the presence of his Father in heaven. Furthermore, unless Jesus was mistaken, the thief also went directly to heaven with him when he died.

It is argued that this could not have been true, for when Jesus appeared to Mary he told her he had not yet ascended to his Father, therefore she must not touch him. On the surface, this seems to make sense, but when we understand the full meaning of this event, we see it in an entirely different light. Mary fell at Jesus' feet and grasped his legs. He said to her in so many words, "Mary, do not hold on to me like that. You have known me in the flesh before this time, but we are not to have that relationship any longer. Your new relationship with me cannot materialize until my ascension to my Father, then you will know me as I dwell within you in the Holy Spirit." The fact is that Jesus Christ entered immediately into the presence of his Father when he died, and there in the holy of holies offered himself the Lamb of God for the sins of the world. The entire Old Testament sacrificial system foreshadowed this great event. Thus, neither Jesus nor the thief entered into soul sleep when they died.

Paul's teachings on this subject agree with what Jesus taught, that is, the soul does not fall into sleep at death, but rather enters into heaven in a conscious state.

He said, "We are of good courage, I say, and are willing rather to be absent from the body, and to be at home with the Lord" (2 Cor 5:8). His own belief is further clarified in the words, "But I am in a strait betwixt the two, having the desire to depart and be with Christ; for it is very far better" (Phil 1:23). Paul did not expect to go to sleep when he died and lie in the tomb until Christ returns; rather, he expected to go immediately into the presence of Christ. If these statements do not convey the truth that the Christian enters into a conscious existence with Christ at death, then words have no meaning.

This truth is further substantiated in Paul's assurance that those who are dead are now with Christ. He wrote the Thessalonians that when Christ returns, he will bring the spirits of the dead with him (1 Thess 4:14). Here Paul used the term "sleep" in speaking of physical death, yet at the same time, he said that Christ will bring them with him when he comes; it is not that he will come and awaken them from soul sleep. The bodies are asleep and will be raised, but the spirits of the redeemed dead are with Christ and will be brought with him when he returns to earth to be given a resurrection body.

The whole theory of soul sleep denies these plain statements of Scripture, choosing rather to deduce beliefs from a materialistic interpretation of certain statements found in the Bible. The old adage that anything can be proven by the Bible is true if we allow just any interpretation of biblical statements to be the basis of that proof. A person can take one word from a scriptural statement, interpret that word to fit his theories, and then go on to interpret other Scriptures in the light of his misinterpretation of that one word, and when he is finished, he has "proved" his theory. We must not follow that method. The teachings of Jesus and Paul are sufficient for our belief that at death a Christian enters into heaven in a conscious condition.

Another theory holds that souls do not enter directly into heaven but are kept in an intermediate place between earth and heaven in preparation for heaven. This is the doctrine of purgatory. The Catholic Church teaches that when a human soul dies it is not fit to enter into the presence of God even though the person may be a Christian. They reason that God is perfect, absolutely so, and therefore, heaven must be a place where only perfection can exist. Because of this, nothing will ever be allowed to enter heaven that is imperfect to any degree. We know that no human being ever reaches this peak of perfection in this life, so at death, every Christian is unfit to enter into God's presence because of his imperfection. To Catholic theologians, this necessitates a period of cleansing and perfecting after death, which in turn, calls for a place between physical death and entrance into heaven where the souls of men can be made perfect. This place is called purgatory, for in it imperfection is purged away and the soul is made fit for heaven. The purifying process consists primarily of some kind of suffering, for suffering is the most effective means of purifying.

According to Catholic teaching, purgatory is not a place where all souls go at death and where they await the decision as to their eternal destiny; eternal destiny is determined before physical death. Purgatory is only for the saved; an unbeliever would never get to purgatory, so it has no power to change an unbeliever into a believer. The length of time an individual would need to remain in purgatory would depend upon how much was brought to bear upon him and how quickly he responded in being purged from imperfection.

This entire concept of the need for some kind of purging after physical death overlooks what God does for a believer in and through Jesus Christ. When a person accepts Jesus Christ as Savior, he is declared perfect in Christ; Jesus Christ becomes his perfect righteousness. Paul wrote in 1 Corinthians 1:30: "But of him are ye in Christ Jesus, who was made unto us wisdom from God, and righteousness and sanctification, and redemption." Paul's doctrine of justification is that when a person receives Jesus Christ by faith, God declares him no longer guilty but forever righteous in Christ. His standing before God is as though he had never committed sin.

One might urge that although a believer is justified in this life before he dies, yet during his life on earth, he still had his carnal nature and is far from being perfectly righteous. This is true, but in physical death man's carnal nature ceases to be a part of his person; it is not the man as he was in the flesh that enters heaven; it is the new man in Christ who has become a new creation who enters the presence of God at physical death. In this life the redeemed soul is inseparably tied in with the carnal nature, but at the death of the body, this carnal nature will cease to be a part of the believer, and he will have finally and completely realized Paul's expressed victory: "Wretched man that I am! who shall deliver me out of the body of this death? I thank God through Jesus Christ our Lord" (Rom 7:24-25).

In physical death the believer will be relieved of all that is imperfect; his spiritual stature or growth will not be affected, as we have already stated, but he will be delivered forever from all possession, practice, and presence of the sin element that was so much a part of his person while he was living in the physical body.

Cleansing from sin for a human soul is the work of Jesus Christ, and this work cannot be done after one has died. The righteousness without which no man can stand before God is that righteousness which is in Jesus Christ by faith; it is not attained by works or through suffering or by any other means except faith.

A person in Jesus Christ is perfect before God. When the fallen nature and sin cease for the individual at death, then the redeemed soul is perfect in Christ and all that constitutes his person partakes of the absolute perfection of Jesus Christ. Otherwise, there would be no hope for any human soul, for the believer's hope is in Jesus Christ and never in himself. Personal righteousness and spiritual growth are important and will be discussed later, but neither is attained after physical death.

Our answer to the question, "Is there an intermediate place between physical death and the resurrection of the body where human souls await the resurrection?" is that there is

not. Believers enter immediately into heaven at death and unbelievers enter directly into hell. We are not to conclude from
this that either the saved or the lost person will enter into his
eternal status at death, for the judgment will come later; but all
human souls do go to either heaven or hell when they die. We
shall discuss this further when we come to the subject of the
judgment and what will take place there. For now we are
saying that there is no in-between place where human souls
to await the resurrection. There is no evidence that there are
more than three possible places where human souls can exist
when the Bible is correctly understood; those places are: on
earth, in heaven, or in hell. Every statement in the Bible when
rightly understood is in harmony with this claim.

Our conclusion is that there is no sleep of the soul after
death, nor is there an intermediate place where souls await
the resurrection and judgment. When we die, we either enter
immediately into the presence of God or we awake, as did the
rich man, in hell, totally separated from God. There is neither
a long journey to heaven, nor is there a stop-over. Some people argue that those who have died for a brief period and then
have been revived, do not remember having been in heaven,
so what we have just said cannot be true. That is, they could
not have gone to heaven immediately, for if they had, they
would remember that experience. What we said about this
under our discussion of soul sleep applies to this objection.
Those who have been resuscitated after having died have
simply had all memory of what happened to them erased.

Having established that the Christian soul enters heaven
immediately after physical death, what can we say about the
state in which that soul exists? The usual concept is that of a
disembodied spirit awaiting the resurrection of the body at
Christ's return to earth. We derive this belief primarily from
Paul's writings.

The fact of the resurrection of the body at the return of
Christ is clearly and fully stated in Scripture. The entire
fifteenth chapter of 1 Corinthians is devoted to this subject.
Having established the fact of the resurrection by the example
of Jesus Christ raised from the dead, Paul went on to say that

Christ was "the first-fruits from the dead" (v. 20) and then gave the order of resurrection: "Christ the first-fruits, then they that are Christ's at his coming" (v. 23). He stated the same truth in 1 Thessalonians 4:13-18, saying there that Christians who have died before Christ returns will come with him when he returns to earth and their bodies will be "raised from the dead" at that time. Without any question, Paul taught that the resurrection of the body will occur at the second coming of Jesus Christ.

These Scriptures appear to indicate that the Christian soul will await the resurrection in heaven in a disembodied state. In 2 Corinthians 5:1-4, however, Paul seems to contradict himself and to state that he expected to receive his resurrection body immediately after death. We believe that all of Scripture, and thus all of Paul's letters, were written under guidance of the Holy Spirit, so there must be a way to resolve this apparent contradiction.

Suppose we see what Paul actually said in 2 Corinthians 5:1-4 by examining his words as though we did not have the statements in 1 Corinthians and 1 Thessalonians. In order to understand this passage it is necessary to keep in mind what Paul had already said in 2 Corinthians 4:7-18. There he referred to our physical bodies as "earthen vessels" (v.7) and to the physical body as "our outward man," noting that it is decaying, that is dying (v. 16). Then in 5:1 he went on to speak of the physical body as "the earthly house of our tabernacle." It is important to note that the word translated "if" in 2 Corinthians 5:1 does not question the fact that he knew he would die. The word used can also mean "when," and that is clearly what Paul intended to say; he knew he would die. So what we are looking for is what Paul said would follow his death.

Let us see first what he said "we have." Paul called it "a building from God, a house not made with hands, eternal in the heavens." Without question he was speaking of his eternal body. Note also that he spoke in the present tense: "When we die, we have then . . ." (author's translation). He *expected* to enter into this new dwelling when he must leave his earthly tabernacle and stated in verse 2 that "verily we groan, longing to be clothed upon with our habitation which is from heaven." He went on to say that his desire was not just to be rid of the old "habitation" but to move into the new. Paul had no desire to be naked, that is without a suitable body in which to live. He said specifically in 5:4 that he groaned, not to be rid of his physical body, "not for that we would be unclothed, but that we would be clothed upon." This clearly refers to his spiritual body, the only kind of body fitted for heaven. It seems clear that Paul did not think in terms of an intermediate state in which he would be without a body.

How could Paul, writing under the guidance of the Holy Spirit, say such contradictory things? Perhaps Paul was not contradicting himself; perhaps he was speaking from two different points of view.

There is one fact of which all Christians are assured: when we die, we will go immediately into God's presence in heaven, to enter into eternity out of and done with this realm of time and space in which we now live. We cannot really conceptualize how this will be for it transcends our powers of imagination. On earth we are creatures of space and time, but in heaven we shall have entered into eternity where neither time nor space exists. God deals with us in time, the time in which we live, but God is not a prisoner of time and space. God is present everywhere and every when. Everything with God is as though it were a colossal NOW. (We cannot really comprehend this fact, but we see it demonstrated when Revelation 13:8 calls Christ "the Lamb slain from the foundation of the world," and it is implied throughout the Bible.) When we die and enter into God's presence in heaven, we too shall be in eternity, and all that was future to us in this world will have become eternal and present to us even as it already has to God. From this viewpoint, there is no reason to think that our spiritual bodies will not already be ours in which to dwell forever and ever.

The problem of reconciling immediate possession of our resurrection bodies with the clear revelation that our bodies are to be raised to incorruption when Christ returns remains.

One of the clearest statements in God's word is that in the end of time God "will judge the world in righteousness by that man whom he hath ordained; whereof he hath given assurance unto all men, in that he has raised him from the dead" (Acts 17:31). Paul also stated (Phil 2:9ff.), "Wherefore, also God highly exalted him and gave unto him a name which is above every name; that at the name of Jesus every knee should bow, of things in heaven [possibly those who will have died before this time] and things on earth and things under earth [could this be the damned in hell?], and that every tongue should confess that Jesus Christ is Lord, to the glory of God." This seems to require that all human beings from Adam to the last person born before Christ returns must be present. Where except on earth could this event take place? People who have not been regenerated cannot possibly enter into heaven for such judgment. Thus the judgment, evidently, must take place on earth, and that means time and space.

And what does all this have to do with our subject? It is this. Since all human creatures are to be judged by God in time and space, all will return to earth for that great public event. The redeemed in heaven, who exist in the NOW of eternity, will return in spirit to have their bodies raised in TIME and SPACE. We cannot be dogmatic about this explanation, for this is a mystery in the biblical sense, a fact that cannot be understood without divine revelation. But it is certainly possible that Paul wrote the statements in 1 Corinthians 15 and 1 Thessalonians 4:13-18 from the point of view of time and space and that he spoke in 2 Corinthians 5:1-4 from the viewpoint of eternity. What is certain is that whether we receive our spiritual bodies immediately upon our deaths or exist in a disembodied state until the Resurrection, at death the Christian soul goes immediately out of earthly life into the presence of God, where all will be well with both body and soul.

Return Trip to Earth?

*T*he explanation of heaven as a realm of spiritual existence coexisting with our material universe opens the way for some extremely dangerous and erroneous speculations. If heaven is this closely related with this world, what about direct communication with the dead? All of us are aware of the emphasis given to the cults in our day. The Bible reveals that some people have always believed in and practiced various forms of occultism; one of the most popular of these has been necromancy, or communication with the dead. Necromancy has become extremely popular in our current society. Spiritualist mediums are thriving on their claims to communicate with the spirits of the dead. Evidently they are reaping abundantly from their fees for their sessions and the popularity their books are being given. The human heart is easily taken advantage of when it comes to this serious matter of some way to continue our earthly relations with our departed loved ones. Sorrow, loneliness, and emptiness, coupled with ignorance of God's truth, and superstition, can create a situation that is ripe for all kinds of deluding claims by those who prey on people's misfortunes.

It has been well said that when true Christianity wanes and people get away from the truth of God, they always become easy victims of all manner of false substitutes for that truth. If this is true, modern society in our nation has gone far astray from God's truth, as the prevalence of astrology and all kinds of occultism would prove. It is not strange that this would be true, but it is rather surprising that many of these cults claim to be Christian and seek to establish their beliefs and practices by the teachings of the Bible. Because of this, we must give some time to this matter of whether the dead can communicate between heaven and earth in general, for this is often urged as evidence for necromancy. If we have a true concept of God, we believe that he himself can communicate with people on earth. He is able to make himself known and the Bible gives many instances in which he has done that. We call these contacts of God with men theophanies, or God-manifestations, or appearances. There are hundreds of instances in the Bible in which God either appeared in some form to man or he spoke in some way to someone. He walked and talked with Adam and Eve in the garden. He communicated with Noah. He appeared to Moses in a burning bush. Often he spoke to men in dreams or visions. Perhaps the most frequent manner in which God communicated with men was through his messengers, the angels. In fact, this is the meaning of the word "angel," God's messenger.

Those of us who accept the Bible as God's revelation of truth raise no question as to the reality of these manifestations of God to men. However, many of us are not convinced that there is any need for modern theophanies. Jesus Christ was and is God's full and final revelation of himself to man. When the Holy Spirit had revealed the full truth of God in Christ to those who wrote the New Testament, there was no further need for special God-manifestations. The Holy Spirit indwells every true Christian and speaks directly through the Word to each one. It is not that God could no longer manifest himself; rather, it is the fact that he no longer needs special manifestations to make himself known. All men today are to come to a knowledge of God through the gospel of Christ; they are to receive it by faith, and are to come to know God through spiritual experience. Jesus had Abram say to the rich man in hell: "They have Moses and the prophets; let them hear them." There are serious questions concerning all claims of special physical and material manifestations of God today.

Really, our desires to have God manifest himself to us in some physical way is almost an insult to the Holy Spirit and a witness to our unwillingness to relate with God by faith. When we are clear on New Testament truth and are willing to enter into a living relationship with God wherein He is accepted and obeyed, we have no need for physical and material proof that he is real, or that he is to be trusted. In the words of Paul, his Spirit bears witness with our spirit that we are his children, and believing this, we rest in his integrity and await the time when all else will be made perfectly clear. Beliefs and practices concerning occultism are not evidences of a true faith in God, but rather a great lack of spiritual reality and a determination to substitute for that reality through naturalistic methods of forcing God to prove himself to us in some physical manner.

What we are saying is not a matter of whether or not God is able to communicate with us today through some special manifestation. Rather, it is saying that there is no longer any need for this method of his revealing himself to us. One day he will again enter into this realm of material substance and make himself visible, for Jesus Christ will one day return to earth and "every eye shall see him." Until that time, we must walk by faith. We must exercise care that we do not allow our imaginations to conjure up some fanciful vision and conclude that God has appeared to us. We must be equally cautious that we do not accept as real the same kind of experience claimed by some other well-meaning person. We can take God at his word and through this exercise of faith, receive all he has for us in this life.

What about communication with the dead? Is it possible for the spirits of the dead to be called back to earth? As we have noted, many spiritualist mediums insist they can communicate with the dead; in fact, they claim they can call back the spirit of a particular person and receive personal messages for the living from him. Quite often, we are told, they produce unquestionable evidences that can be seen or heard by the inquirer. The mediums communicate accurate facts concerning the departed and give information that supposedly only the inquirer himself has. In this manner, they establish their ability to communicate with the dead. They are able to convince people who are under great emotional strain of their claims, for they always tell them what they want to hear. This is usually some trivial matter that has little true value except to confirm the wishes of the person involved. It helps them to close their eyes to realities and to follow an easy-going way of dealing with life's difficulties, according to Dr. E. Y. Mullins, in his little book *Spiritualism, A Delusion*.

When we study the Bible on this subject, we find no encouragement whatsoever that the dead can communicate with
the living. In fact, the Bible repeatedly condemns all forms of
divination and necromancy. There are several words used in
the Bible in speaking of some form of communicating with the
spirits. "Divination" was applied to any false means of discovering the divine will. All such means as using divining
rods (Hos 4:12), arrows (Ezek 21:21), and consulting oracles
(Isa 61:21-24) are condemned. "Augury" was one form of divination in which objects were used such as birds, stars, cards,
dice, or dregs in a cup to obtain the message, followed by the
uttering of the message received. The word "sorcerer" or
"sorceress" meant the same thing (Exod 22:18; Jer 27:9-10; Mal
3:5). Astrological pronouncements constitute modern augury
or sorcery. An "enchanter" was a person who used a "song
spell," or serpent charming, or some other form of magical
speel to get his message. The word means to hiss or whisper
as a serpent. A "consulter of familiar spirits" was one who
claimed to be bound with some spirit. This kind of receiving
special knowledge was usually connected with evil spirits. A
"wizard" was a man who claimed to do what a witch is
supposed to do. He could interpret the ravings of a medium.
A "witch" was the same as a sorceress. As we have already
noted, a "necromancer" was one who inquired of the dead
and claimed to communicate with them and to receive messages from them to give to others.

All forms and practices of these types of magic were
considered polytheistic in nature and condemned as idolatrous by the true prophets of God. Moses strictly forbade such
practices. He included most of the terms used of these practices in Deuteronomy 18:10-12: "There shall not be found with
thee any one that maketh his son or daughter to pass through
the fire, one that useth divination, one that practiceth augury,
or an enchanter, or a consulter with familiar spirits, or a
wizard, or a necromancer. For whosoever doeth these things
is an abomination unto Jehovah." He wrote in Leviticus 19:31,
"Turn ye not unto them that have familiar spirits, nor unto
the wizards; seek them not out, to be defiled by them: I am

Jehovah your God." In the same book he wrote, "And the soul that turneth unto them that have familiar spirits, and unto the wizards, to play the harlot after them, I will even set my face against that soul, and will cut him off from among his people (20:6).

Isaiah soundly condemned all idolatrous seeking after those who claimed special powers. He wrote, "And when they shall say unto you, Seek unto them that have familiar spirits and unto the wizards that chirp and mutter: should not a people seek unto their God? On behalf of the living should they seek unto the dead? To the law and testimony! If they speak not according to this word, surely there is no morning for them." One could hardly find condemnation of any practice clearer or more to the point than is expressed in these statements. This is clearly the case throughout the Old Testament.

In the New Testament we find the same condemnation of these practices we have in the Old Testament. In the English translations, two words are used in the New Testament that refer to this practice. The first one is the word from which we get our word "magic." It is translated either "wise man" as with the "Wise Men" from the east who visited the baby Jesus in Bethlehem, and it is also translated "magician or sorcerer." The verb is translated "to use magic" or "to practice sorcery." The other Greek word is the word from which we get our English word "pharmacy." It was used to express the practice of enchanting with the use of drugs. There is one use of a word that is translated "divination." The word is the same as that used in Greek mythology of the Pythian serpent or dragon.

Let us note well the attitude of New Testament writers regarding the people who practiced these magical arts. In Acts 8:9-24 we have the account of Simon the sorcerer in Samaria. Under the preaching of Philip, the deacon, Simon, a very popular sorcerer, pretended to accept Jesus Christ and was baptized. However, when Peter came to Samaria, and after praying, laid his hands on the disciples, the Holy Spirit came upon them. This made such an impression on Simon that he offered to pay Peter to give him the secret of such magic.

Peter's response to this request reflects the general attitude of New Testament writers toward all kinds of sorcery and magic. He said, "Repent therefore of this thy wickedness, and pray the Lord, if perhaps the thought of thy heart shall be forgiven thee. For I see that thou art in the gall of bitterness and in the bond of iniquity" (Acts 8:22-23). In other words, Peter strongly branded the practice of sorcery as strictly contrary to the meaning and spirit of true Christianity. It is also evident that he considered this man as totally outside the experience of God's saving grace. There is no reason to believe that he would consider all such practices any different today.

A similar situation developed for Paul on the Island of Cyprus on his first missionary journey. Paul and Barnabas were witnessing to the governor of the island when a sorcerer named Elymas interfered with what they were saying, evidently in an effort to defeat their purpose. Paul took the matter in hand and said to Elymas, "O full of all guile and villainy, thou son of the devil, thou enemy of all righteousness, wilt thou not cease to pervert the right ways of the Lord? And now, behold, the hand of the Lord is upon thee, and thou shalt be blind, not seeing the sun for a season. And immediately there fell on him a mist and a darkness; and he went about seeking someone to lead him by the hand" (Acts 13:10-11). Paul connected such practices with the devil and branded them as contrary to the truth. Elymas was exercising his powers in an effort to pervert the truth of God and to feather his own nest. The truth has not changed since Paul had this run-in with Elymas; these things are contrary to God, to his truth, and to his ways of working with men.

When Paul and his missionary group came to Phillipi on his second journey, they were troubled by a young girl who had a spirit of divination. The word used here is the one referred to above, "python." She was said to have brought her masters gain by soothsaying. This word "soothsaying" is derived from the same word found in the compound word "necromancer." It means to seek to know so as to predict future things by resorting to the spirits. She did not confer with the dead, but relied on her powers of divination from contact with evil spirits. Paul cast out the evil spirit and she was healed. This practice of divination is ascribed to demon possession and the divining she did was derived from the evil spirit that controlled her.

The word translated "sorcery" and derived from the Greek word that means to use drugs is used only in the book of Revelation. It is used four times (9:21; 18:23; 21:8; 22:15), and in every use, the practice is condemned. In 21:8, the statement is made that sorcerers, along with a number of others, will have their part in the lake that burns with fire and brimstone. In 22:15, sorcerers are classified with the vilest of sinners: "dogs, and the sorcerers, and the fornicators, and the murderers, and the idolaters, and every one that maketh and loveth a lie." It is difficult to see how anyone could claim to be a Christian while practicing any of these magical arts, when the New Testament is so strong in its condemnation of such practices.

Yet, there are some who do just that. In order to justify their practices of communicating with the dead, they claim biblical sanction and examples in the Bible where it was approved. In discussing the idea of the communication of the dead with the living, let us keep in mind that we are not speaking about God's communication with men. We have already dealt with that subject. What we have in mind now is whether the Bible can be used as the basis for any claim that a human being who has died can in any way communicate with the living on earth. Can those who claim to have the powers to receive messages from the dead justify their claims by citing biblical teachings? It would seem that with all the teachings against these practices, there would be no further questions. The Bible does not strongly condemn a practice in one place and then approve that same practice in another place.

There is one thing for sure concerning the teachings of the Bible on any subject; when it is correctly understood, it is consistent in its teachings. We can be safe interpreting any particular passage that may be difficult as being in harmony with the general teachings of the Bible on that subject.

There are many statements in the Bible that can be distorted and by so doing, it is possible to inject ideas of all kinds, including the possibility of communing with the dead. We cannot deal with this kind of claimed evidence. There are several events in the Bible that are used to substantiate claims that this practice is approved by biblical writers. Perhaps the most common is the experience of Saul and the witch of Endor. The account is given in 1 Samuel 28. The situation is that Samuel had died and Saul was left without any one to counsel him. He was the type of man who required some special mystical encouragement to bolster up his actions; he could not make decisions on his own. Under attack from the Philistines, things looked pretty dark. Since he could not communicate with God, he sought out the witch of Endor and constrained her to call up Samuel from the dead. This she presumably did and gave Saul a message from him. Many people believe this to have been a real instance in which the dead did communicate with the witch, but there are several aspects of the account that cause us to reject it as real.

As we have said, the general condemnation of the practice would render it as contrary to God's way of dealing with men, so here is a strike against its being real before we consider anything else. Besides this, God had refused to communicate with Saul when he inquired of him, so why should he have anything to do with the witch, and why should he do through her what he had refused to do directly? (v. 6). Again, it is not said that Saul ever saw Samuel, only the witch claimed to see him. She would describe him as she knew he would be dressed, so there is no evidence here that she really saw him. Whatever else we might say about mediums, we must not forget they are cunning and able to make things appear foolproof and real. Neither did Saul hear Samuel speak; he only assumed that she heard him. Under circumstances like this, charged with intense emotion, Saul quickly jumped to the very conclusions the witch intended.

There are some other problems in accepting this as real. Samuel had totally turned away from Saul before he died; why then should he return to earth to do what he refused to do while alive? It is likely that Samuel was true to the law of Moses and had urged God's people to refrain from all idolatry such as seeking to communicate with the dead. Again, why should he after death go contrary to what God had forbidden? It is unthinkable that he would to this.

Someone might argue that the message the witch gave Saul came true. The fact is that only part of it came true. She said that Saul and his sons would be with Samuel the next day; not all of Saul's sons were slain with him. Any person with the powers of this witch could know the serious situation caused by the Philistines and could predict Saul's death, so there is no proof to be derived from what she said.

There are some people who believe that this incident was the one exception in which God turned aside from his usual way of doing things in order to teach Saul a lesson. In the light of all other teachings on this kind of thing, to me, this is unthinkable. God never resorts to wrongdoing for any purpose. He would never encourage, or approve, or have a part in anything that is as clearly idolatry as is necromancy. He has other ways of teaching men lessons than resorting to practices totally condemned in all other instances. The psalmist wrote, "The works of his hands are truth and justice;/ All his precepts are sure./ They are established for ever and ever;/ they are done in truth and uprightness" (111:7-8).

There are three possible explanations of what the witch of Endor did. First, it could have been trickery. Saul was in such a state of mind that he could have easily been deluded by her. However, there seems to have been more than deceit involved in this incident. Second, she could have been capable of mental telepathy and could have used this power to give the message to Saul. The third possibility is that she could have exercised demonic powers. Personally, I feel that whatever was real in the calling back of Samuel on this occasion was satanic in origin. This is only a personal opinion, but I believe it harmonizes with all other teachings in the Bible on the subject.

The only other instance in the Bible in which we have some form of communication of the dead with the living was the transfiguration experience of Jesus. We are told that Moses and Elijah appeared to Jesus and talked with him (Matt 17:3). There should be no question as to the authenticity of this experience. At the same time, neither should it be used to substantiate the claim that the dead in general can communicate with the living today. Jesus Christ was a special Person; no Christian would claim to be what he was, or to have the same relationship with the Father he had.

It is equally true that no follower of Christ would claim to do what Jesus did in the work of redemption. The transfiguration of Jesus Christ was a most unusual, indeed a unique, experience that was directly connected in some way with his coming death for sin. Luke said that the three talked of his decease which he was to accomplish at Jerusalem (Luke 9:31). Just what part Moses and Elijah had in this conversation it is impossible to know; we can know that there is not the least indication that similar conversations of the dead with the living are necessary.

It seems likely that Peter may have had some idea that since Jesus communed with Moses and Elijah, Christians would be able to do the same thing, so he proposed that tabernacles, or places of worship, be set up, one each for Jesus, Moses, and Elijah. Jesus did not speak to this proposal, but the Father did, and he did it in no uncertain terms as to what he meant. He told Peter that Jesus Christ, his Son, was to be the center and only concern of his children, "This is my beloved Son, in whom I am well pleased; hear ye him" (Matt 17:5). In other words, "Do not think to commune with Moses and Elijah, or with any other person from the dead; you hear and heed the words of my Son!"

It is the height of presumption to think that since Moses and Elijah communed with Jesus Christ, one can do the same thing with any person who is dead. It is here we discover the idolatrous idea in this matter, which is, to presume to exercise the prerogative of God. Let only the person who feels himself to be in the same category with Jesus Christ presume to communicate with the dead, and let him justify his claims by a transfiguration experience of his own.

There is a strong statement against any communication of the dead with the living in Jesus' account of the rich man and Lazarus in Luke 16:19ff. We must recognize there is a difference between the communication of the dead in heaven and the communication of the dead with the living on earth. The rich man asked that Lazarus be sent back to earth to warn his brothers to take whatever steps were necessary to avoid going to hell when they died.

In the answer, two things were said. First, God does not preach the Gospel to the living through the dead. The living have the Word of God, and they must accept the truth by faith if they ever come to be right with God. Even angels were never used to preach the gospel of salvation to lost souls. The second truth is that there is no passing back and forth from heaven to hell or from hell to heaven. In other words, when a human soul once enters into either heaven or hell, he does not go roaming around in any other areas. Whatever the "great gulf" is, it speaks of an uncrossable separation between the place the soul goes at death and any other place. God himself may cross as he pleases, but human souls are not given this power.

What shall we conclude about all the claims of people to communicate with the dead and all the evidence they produce that their communication is authentic? What explanations can be given of the giving out of accurate information concerning the dead in seances, or the appearances of physical forms visible to the living? These matters have been researched carefully by scientific organizations and several pretty reliable conclusions have been suggested.

There are three possibilities that might satisfactorily explain any and all of these "happenings" given by scientific researchers, and there is a fourth possibility that I would suggest. Parapsychology, the science concerned with these investigations, has studied telepathy, clairvoyance, and extra-sensory perception, as possible explanations.

Telepathy is the ability to convey or receive a thought to or from another person without the use of ordinary means of communication; it is direct thought transference from one person to another. Clairvoyance is the power to discern ideas without the use of one of the five senses. It is the claimed ability to perceive or to discern ideas that a person could not otherwise know, including future events. Extrasensory perception is similar to clairvoyance; it means to receive ideas outside the use of one of the five senses. It is usually referred to today as ESP.

Many reports have been written and published containing the findings of scientific research. Experiments have been made and the general conclusion reached is that mental tele-pathy is a recognized fact and that it alone can explain the unusual things spiritual mediums pass on to their clients. Mediums are capable of reading the minds of the people who come to them and give messages on the bases of what they derive in this manner. Even the hopes and plans of people can be detected in this way, and future events can be predicted. The subconscious mind may retain plans that have been for-gotten by the conscious mind and pass them on to mediums by mental telepathy, or even a dream may thus be conveyed to a medium. It is likely that much of what passes as proof of communication with the dead is nothing more than informa-tion derived through teleplay. The vast possibilities of this kind of thing is only beginning to be investigated and understood.

The fourth possibility mentioned above is that satanic powers must be considered a possible explanation of some of the manifestations by spiritual mediums. This would not be acceptable to scientific groups as such, but the teachings of the Bible definitely support it. We do not believe Satan exercises omnipotence; however, he is able to perform superhuman deeds that would appear as miraculous. Paul stated this clearly in speaking of the coming of the man of sin, "...whose coming is according to the working of Satan with all power and signs and lying wonders, and with all deceit of unrighteousness for them that perish; because they received not the love of the truth, that they might be saved" (2 Thess 2:9-10).

I feel we may be safe in concluding that any and all manifestations purporting to be communications with the dead can be explained either as deceit and trickery, or as the result of using mental telepathy, or as the exercise of satanic or demonic powers. As has been explained, we can be definitely sure that the Bible condemns all forms of these practices and forbids God's children to have anything to do with them. Isaiah's admonition is still applicable to God's people of our day, "Should not a people seek unto their God?" A genuine and close relationship with God is the solution to problems with this practice. This relationship will also meet every true need we may have regarding what we need to know about heaven and life after death.

There is another theory in which the claim is made that a human soul can return to earth after death; it is called the reincarnation or transmigration of the soul. According to the *Encyclopedia Americana*, transmigration has been taught as far back in history as we have any account. It was held by the Brahmanic Hindus, the earliest record of it, and it consisted of the idea "of the gradual purification of the spiritual part of man and its return to the common source and origin of all things-God" (see article on "Transmigration").

The difference between transmigration and reincarnation is that transmigration teaches that the soul returns to earth in a lower form, perhaps an animal, or even a plant, if it was unfaithful in its former existence on earth. However, it might return in an improved human soul if it had been faithful. The theory of reincarnation does not teach that the soul returns in animal or plant life, but that it always returns in a human body greater than its former body. The only purpose for reincarnation is for further purification of the soul in preparation for heaven, according to its adherents.

This theory of reincarnation is believed by some sincere people today who have been convinced it is true by false teachers. Several observations need to be made concerning it.

For one thing, there is a strong similarity in the reasoning that leads to this theory and that which is used to teach the place and purpose of purgatory by the Roman Catholic Church. Both hold to the fact that heaven is a perfect place, God is absolute perfection, and therefore, no soul can enter his presence without being perfect. Since no human being becomes perfect before he dies, there must be some way by which he can be perfected so as to enter into heaven eventually. This perfecting is done, according to Catholic teaching, in purgatory. The same thing is accomplished, according to the theory of reincarnation, by the soul's return to earth to improve himself in living another life.

If we were forced to choose between the two theories, we would prefer the Roman Catholic idea, for the simple reason that at least in a place like purgatory, the human soul would be free of the physical body and carnal nature, so might well be purified and made perfect. However, no number of reincarnations could possibly produce a perfect human soul on earth. Thus the very purpose of reincarnation is automatically impossible.

As we noted earlier in discussing purgatory, the idea is arrived at by reasoning, a reasoning that has two flaws. First, it fails to understand the gospel of Christ in which believers are accounted perfectly righteous in Jesus Christ. Thus, when we die and leave the physical body and carnal nature behind, we have our perfect standing before the Father. The other flaw consists in the idea that we attain to perfection by good works. All theological theories that grow from this concept must concoct some method by which man can lift himself by his own bootstraps. The Bible teaches that there is no justification before God on the basis of the works of the Law.

What about the claims that the Bible teaches reincarnation? When the writings of those who hold to this theory are studied, it is found that many of them are frank to admit that the Bible does not directly teach the theory, but that it can easily be read into the Bible statements. Some of them believe that certain words have been changed in meaning, and that these words originally conveyed the idea of reincarnation, but this argument is extremely unreliable.

The truth about the entire idea of reincarnation is that it is derived from ancient religions and is fostered by natural philosophical reasonings in such a way as to support this preconceived idea. If a person would begin with the Bible without previous beliefs derived from other sources, it is highly doubtful that he would ever discover any ideas in the Bible even remotely related with the theory of reincarnation.

Before we examine a few of the statements in the Bible into which ideas of reincarnation are read, let us state briefly some reasonings that lead to the belief itself. It is based upon a complicated analysis of the human soul, including the idea that all human souls were created at the same time. Each soul is given its choice as to what body it will live in on earth in order to attain perfection; from there on out, the series continues until the soul has reached the stage of perfection that will allow it to enter heaven. The origin of the human soul is not known, so the basis of this theory is very uncertain. Many of us are convinced that the soul is the natural result of natural conception, and that it develops along with the embryo in the mother's womb. To say the least, there is no way to know just when the soul originates.

A further idea of the theory of reincarnation is that there is a universal law of Karma by which the soul of man exists and through its many lives, comes to perfection. The basic idea in this law is the principle of cause and effect. The argument is that since this principle prevails in all life, each soul must reach perfection by means of the good done in life; the "repeat performances" in better bodies is the way perfection is finally attained. One can easily see the unjustified jump from a principle of cause and effect to the method claimed in the process of reincarnation. It is also clear that the entire idea of becoming perfect is a matter of self-improvement according to this theory, and gives no place to the grace and work of God in providing righteousness in Jesus Christ. Really, as suggested above, the theory of reincarnation originates in ancient religious philosophies, is developed by naturalistic reasonings, and then, at least for those who want biblical sanction, it is read into certain selected statements in the Bible.

Space forbids a full consideration of this claimed biblical support for reincarnation, so we shall mention only a few to indicate the method used. It is urged by some that the prophecy of Malachi, "Behold, I will send you Elijah the prophet before the great and terrible day of Jehovah come" (4:5), distinctly teaches reincarnation, especially in the light of Jesus' statement concerning John the Baptist. He said, "And if ye are willing to receive it, this is Elijah, that is to come (Matt 11:14). The claim is that John the Baptist was Elijah reincarnate. If this was true, it is rather strange that the angel that spoke to John's father did not know it. In explaining the nature and work of this promised son, the angel said, "And he shall go before his face in the spirit and power of Elijah, to turn the hearts of the fathers to the children" (Luke 1:17). This messenger of God understood the prophecy of Malachi to mean that John the Baptist would not actually be Elijah, reincarnate, but a prophet of God like unto Elijah, possessing and exercising the wisdom and power Elijah had.

In addition to this plain explanation of the angel, we learn in the transfiguration experience of Jesus that Elijah was alive in heaven and still Elijah, for he, along with Moses, appeared to talk with Jesus there. The prophecy of Malachi could only mean that God would prepare the way for the coming of Christ by using a prophet of whom Elijah was a type. A person may as well claim that Jesus was the reincarnation of Moses as to claim that John the Baptist was actually the reincarnation of Elijah. Moses said, "Jehovah thy God will raise up unto thee a prophet from the midst of thee, of thy brethren, like unto me: unto him ye shall hearken" (Deut 18:15). Peter understood that Jesus was this prophet like to Moses (Acts 3:22-26), and so did Stephen (Acts 7:37). To claim that Jesus was Moses reincarnated is to deny that Jesus Christ is the eternal Son of God. Furthermore, if John was actually Elijah reincarnate, he himself was not aware of it. When the priests and Levites asked him if he was Elijah, he replied, "I am not." It is not difficult to see what distortion of scriptural statement is made in an effort to establish biblical backing for the theory of reincarnation.

An effort to establish the system of Karma is made by using Jesus' statement that his followers would be able to do greater works than he had done. The plea is made that this would be possible only if men become perfect as Jesus was. This, in turn, requires many returns through the method of reincarnation, for making one perfect is a difficult task. Jesus did not say that any person would ever become perfect in this life, nor did he mean that any person would perform works more miraculous or greater in spiritual quality than he did.

The word "greater" is used in the New Testament with varying shades of meaning; its meaning in this statement of Jesus is that Jesus' disciples, because they would be filled with the same Holy Spirit he was filled with, would be enabled to do much greater, that is, far more extensive works, than he had been able to do. Their works would not depend on their becoming perfect, but rather on the indwelling of the Holy Spirit. The spread of Christianity and its continuing works is the fulfillment of Jesus' promise. It is a far leap in a desperate effort to support a theory to urge this statement as teaching the necessity for reincarnation.

Many other interpretations are given in an effort to harmonize this ancient Oriental theory with biblical truth. The great New Testament truth of the new birth is interpreted in support of the renewal claimed through reincarnation. Some claim that the word for "resurrection" originally carried the meaning of "reincarnation."

One of the most peculiar statements I have found is to the effect that reincarnation is the same teaching as the continuation of life beyond physical existence on earth. With this confusion, the writer proceeded to quote Scriptures to substantiate the New Testament teaching on life after death. It does not require great intellectual capacity or spiritual discernment to know that there is a vast difference between reincarnation and the biblical doctrine of life beyond physical death. In reading the contentions of those who try to prove by the Bible that reincarnation is a correct idea, a person who does any thinking at all is struck with the great gaps existing in their proofs and the weak implications they make. They succeed only in pointing to statements that might, by straining the imagination, leave a tiny possibility of crowding the idea in. Why go outside the Word of God for beliefs that are not in that Word, and then try to make corrections in the Bible in an effort to substantiate those beliefs? No ancient religious theories or philosophical ideas are worthy such diligent defense.

There is an appealing argument that is urged in defense of the theory of reincarnation to the effect that all of us have a strange sensation at times that we have been here before. The poets have sung of echoes that come to us from the distant shores. This is a common experience with many people. However, no proof exists in this experience that we have been here before in some other form. It is proof only of the powers of the subconscious mind or of some dream long ago. To say the least, all such impressions can be explained from a natural or psychological viewpoint. Again, all such reasonings are weak support for the theory of reincarnation.

If the claims of those who believe in reincarnation are true, it is inexplicably strange that the Bible does not clearly present the idea. We cannot imagine that such an important idea, if true, would be only remotely contained in the bible, and even then it would need to be implied from statements on other subjects. This is the best that can be done in trying to find biblical teachings to support the idea; it is not enough for people who have come to know God through faith in his clearly revealed truth. This is doubly true in the light of the multiplied plain scriptural statements that teach a "one time only" chance at life, the finality of physical death so far as change is concerned, and the fact that the Christian enters directly and permanently into heaven when he dies. Jesus Christ is our one and only hope for ever being right with God.

We who have come to know him are persuaded that he is completely sufficient to present us faultless before God when we leave this life. Paul wrote, "Husbands, love your wives, even as Christ also loved the church, and gave himself up for it; that he might sanctify it, having cleansed it by the washing of water with the word, that he might present the church to himself a glorious church, not having spot or wrinkle or any such thing; but that it should be holy and without blemish" (Eph 5:25-27). He states the same truth as it applies to the individual, "Yet now hath he reconciled in the body of his flesh through death, to present you holy and without blemish and unreprovable before him" (Col 1:22). There is no place for being made perfect according to the laws of Karma in reincarnation in this statement. It is the death of Jesus Christ that reconciles men to God and renders them holy and without blemish and unreprovable before him. We are to grow in the grace and knowledge of Jesus Christ; we are to become as spiritually mature as we can; yet, at the same time, our only hope of standing before our Holy God in absolute perfection is in Jesus Christ.

The only return trip from heaven to earth will be made by Jesus Christ when he comes the second time. He will bring with him all the redeemed to receive their resurrection bodies (see 1 Thess 4:13ff.). Until that time, heaven's communication with people on earth is by means of the Holy Spirit and he does not resort to physical manifestations. His is the "still small voice" speaking to the inner man. His speaking is always in harmony with the Word of God, and most always through that Word. Knowing him and being able to commune with him, we do not need psychological or satanic help; *he* is our helper. With him as our helper, we believe Paul's word of assurance to the Ephesians, "Now unto him that is able to do exceeding abundantly above all that we ask or think, according to the power that worketh in us" (3:20).

What about Hell?

*W*e have reached a point in our study that requires a discussion of hell. Many questions likely have been raised in the reader's mind concerning hell as we have discussed this view of heaven. If heaven is a spiritual place, coexisting with our material universe, what about hell? "Where on earth is hell?" might well be a question parallel with the subject of this book.

Before seeking an answer to this question, let us say a word about the teaching of the Bible on the reality of hell. Man's natural mind loathes the idea of hell and prefers to believe either that death is the end of existence, or that somehow, all human beings will eventually get to heaven. The argument is used, often by theologians, that any idea of hell as a place of eternal punishment is contrary to the concept of a God of love. They claim that God would never prepare such a place for man because he loves all men and could never do such a thing to any creature. They attribute all teachings on hell to men who are misguided and do not understand a God of love.

Two things need to be determined about this contention. First, does the fact that God is love forbid hell? Second, what does the Bible teach concerning hell? We would say the same thing about the reality of hell that we say about the reality of heaven: we cannot prove it. However, it is equally true that neither can we disprove it. No Christian delights in the thoughts of hell for any human soul. In fact, many of us do not believe the subject of hell should ever be treated lightly or made the basis of a joke. It is far too serious a subject for us to make light of it, or to wish it for anyone. It is not man's prerogative to decide whether or not there is a hell, nor to determine who is to go there. Thus we are to find answers to our questions in the Bible. What men think or wish about the matter of hell cannot serve as a solid basis for our belief.

Let us consider whether or not the fact that God is love means there cannot be such a place as hell. The claim is that since God is love, He is too good to allow such a place to exist. Our answer requires a restatement of the meaning of the word "love" as applied to God. We have said that it means a total otherness. It means that God does not need anything for himself as a Being and that his only desire for man is to give himself to man for man's own eternal good.

The love of God for man is in no way a sentimental quality that would pamper any creature regardless of matters of holiness and righteousness. It is God's desire to do for man and give to man that which is for his true good. However, we must keep in mind that when God created man, he gave him the freedom of choice; this included the freedom and power to determine for himself how he would be related with God. God does not want a relationship with any intelligent creature that is forced upon that creature. This would be contrary to the true meaning of love.

Since there is no true freedom apart from responsibility for the use of that freedom, man was made responsible for the way he chose to relate with God. If he chooses to relate rightly with God, then he becomes a child of God and God is able to give himself to man with all the joys of a happy life on earth and the blessedness of eternity in heaven. When a free human being uses his freedom to reject the truth of God and to refuse to relate rightly with him, then there is no alternative except to allow him to do so. In making this choice, man becomes responsible for the results of separation from God. He lives his life in this world without God, and when he dies, God will not pick him up against his will and drag him into a place so drastically different from the kind of person he has chosen to become.

My personal belief is that if an unregenerate human soul should be taken into heaven when he dies, it would be worse for him than hell would be. Besides this, heaven is a place of eternal spiritual life; the unregenerate human soul does not have spiritual life, so it is impossible for any soul to enter into heaven without being born again. This is what Jesus told

Nicodemus in speaking of the absolute necessity for being born again (John 3). A spiritually dead person cannot live in a place of spiritual life. All the sentimental claims that God will eventually take everybody to heaven anyway does not make sense in the light of these things.

Someone will likely object, "But how could a God of love prepare such a place as hell?" The answer is that there must be some place for creatures to spend eternity who are determined not to spend it with God. People who are not willing for God to become a part of their existence must be allowed to exist in a place separate and apart from God: we call this place hell.

We are mistaken if we think God delights in sending even rebellious creatures to hell. Peter said that God does not wish for any to perish, but He desires that all men should come to repentance (2 Pet 3:9). Paul wrote that God would have all men to be saved and to come to the knowledge of the truth (1 Tim 2:4). However, man is free to go contrary to God's wishes, and when he does, God has no alternative but to allow him to have his own way and to suffer the consequences.

The fact is that hell has not been provided primarily for man. Jesus said it was prepared for the devil and his angels (Matt 25:41). Someone has suggested that a human being in hell will be an intruder. If he goes to hell, he will certainly do it contrary to God's desires for him. It has been suggested that God has fenced hell in to discourage all men from going there. All that he has done in redeeming sinful man from sin could well be considered as fencing it in. We must remember that all men are free to choose for themselves, and when they make their choices contrary to all that God is and has done, then God is no longer to be saddled with the blame.

In addition to the fact that the true meaning of the love of God does not forbid the existence of an eternal hell where unregenerate human souls go at death, it is also to be kept in mind that God's love in no way conflicts with his holiness and righteousness. He is a holy God. This holiness characteristic includes all the other moral qualities of God. As a holy God, he is also just and righteous. God is as bound by his holy nature to deal in justice with sinful man as he is inclined by nature to deal with repentant man in grace and mercy. God's holy nature is repulsed by all evil; he by his very holiness of being responds to all unholiness with repugnance. Although he does love a sinful man and has done everything possible to save him, he still has a holy aversion to man's sinfulness and he will deal in justice with every human being who rejects his love. Paul argues that the only way a holy and just God can forgive and save a guilty sinner is because Jesus Christ died for sin (see Rom 3:25-26).

Outside of Jesus Christ, there is no provision for sin, and God has no choice but to deal in perfect justice. Since the wages of sin is death, justice requires that the unrepentant soul receive in full what he deserves. Eternal separation from a holy God is the only destiny possible for a human being who rejects the love of God in Jesus Christ.

Now let us consider the teachings of the Bible on the reality of hell. First, the teachings of the Old Testament on hell must be understood in the same light that we have considered its teachings on life after death and heaven. We have said that the details about existence after physical death are not revealed in the Old Testament. The word *sheol*, as we have noted, is the one word used in speaking of the abode of the dead, both righteous and unrighteous. We must determine by the context whether it is to be translated as hell; it is used with this meaning thirty-one times according to Young's *Analytical Concordance to the Bible*.

In the New Testament three different words are translated "hell." The Greek word that corresponds with *sheol* is *hades*. It basically means the abode of the dead, and is translated in the New Testament as hell ten times; it is translated as the grave one time.

The word Jesus used is *gehenna*. It is used twelve times in the entire New Testament, and eleven of those are attributed to Jesus: James used it in his epistle one time (3:6). This word is a transliteration into Greek of the Hebrew words *ge* and *hinnom*. It means "the Valley of Hinnom." This was a valley just south of Jerusalem. It had gotten its name *hinnom* from the fact that the word means "lamentation." Prior to 640 B.C., the Jews had erected a temple to the fire god, Moloch. Part of the worship was to lay a baby in the arms of this idol that had been heated by fire within the idol. This brought about screams from the babies and wailings from the mothers; thus, the place received its name.

Josiah, king of Judah, destroyed the temple and forbade all worship of the fire god. The place where the temple had stood was cursed and made a garbage dumping place. All kinds of refuse was cast into this place, along with the dead bodies of dogs and other animals. In order to maintain as high a degree of sanitation as possible, fires were kept constantly burning. In spite of this, maggots were always infesting the dead carcasses in the pit. The place came to be called "the gehenna of fire." This is the term Jesus used in speaking of hell.

We do not know whether others had used the word in referring hell, but we do know that Jesus used it that way. He urged that men do anything that was necessary to avoid being cast into "gehenna" when they die, describing that place further "where their worm dieth not and the fire is not quenched" (Mark 9:48). It is clearly evident that Jesus believed and taught the reality of hell as the eternal abode of unbelievers.

There is one other word in the New Testament that was used in referring to hell. It is *tartaroo*. This word is translated "to cast down to hell" and is used only one time in the New Testament (2 Pet 2:4). It was a purely Greek word used to denote the subterranean regions where the evil go when they die. It carried the same meaning for the Greeks that *gehenna* had for the Jews, according to Thayer's *Lexicon*.

These three words that mean hell are used twenty-three times in the New Testament. In addition to these words, hell is referred to in a number of other words or terms. Jesus used the terms, "eternal fire" (Matt 18:8; 25:41); "eternal damnation" (Mark 3:29); "hell fire" (Matt 18:9); "furnace of fire" (Matt 13:42,50); and "eternal punishment" (Matt 25:46). In the book of Revelation, hell is spoken of as "a lake of fire" (19:20;

20:10,14-15; 21:8). "Fire and brimstone" is also used in Revelation 14:10; 19:20; 20:10; and 21:8.

From these teachings in the New Testament, we must conclude either that hell is a real place, or that the writers of the New Testament were deluded. This includes Jesus Christ, for he evidently believed in its reality and warned against it. The truth is that we have as much basis for believing in hell as we do for believing in heaven. It is not a matter of what we would like to believe; rather, we accept the Bible as the authority on these matters, and it definitely teaches the reality of hell.

A brief word needs to be written concerning the claim that a lost soul is annihilated at death. Statements like "shall not perish" of John 3:16, "eternal destruction" in Paul's statement in 2 Thessalonians 1:8, are used to substantiate this teaching. Terms like these do not teach the annihilation of the soul; they carry the meaning of utter ruin and degradation, along with the loss of all that is good. The fact that the Bible plainly teaches that lost souls will spend eternity in hell requires this interpretation. It is not that lost souls will be eternally destroyed and thus pass out of existence. Rather, the idea is that they shall enter into a place of utter ruin where they will spend eternity; a place, according to Jesus, "where the worm dieth not and the fire is not quenched."

Now let us return to the problem confronted in the opening paragraph of this section: where is hell and what kind of place is it? In the light of our belief that heaven is a realm of spiritual reality co-existing with our material universe, what conclusion shall we reach concerning hell? Hell is another realm of existence that is non-material in nature and that co-exists with heaven and this material universe. All three realms exist without one of them necessarily interfering with or affecting the other. Our universe is a realm of material substances; heaven is a realm of spiritual life and realities; hell is a realm of death and darkness, the opposite of heaven. While the material universe is temporal and will one day be destroyed, heaven and hell are both eternal in nature.

What we have said about heaven and space can also be said about hell. Hell is not located in some particular place in this universe; it exists outside this realm of space in a way that is not affected in any way by space. It simply transcends space, even as heaven does. Neither is hell composed of material substances. The physical bodies of human beings decay in death and return to the dust of the earth, but the soul continues its existence. The body of the unrepentant will not go into hell when that person dies; it remains in the grave as we can plainly see. Thus, hell is a realm of nonmaterial reality where the soul of man enters at death if he has not been born again with the life of God. The nature of hell must be such that the nonphysical person experiences its qualities. It must also be of such nature that it is eternal, for hell is referred to as eternal in nature (Jude 7).

Let us remind ourselves that this fact about hell in no way indicates that it is imaginary or unreal. Hell is as real as heaven; both are eternally real. For the time being, we must speak of both heaven and hell in the only words we have. We must adapt our vocabulary of material terms to realms of non-material realities, while retaining the meaning as best we can of those realities. Let us seek to describe what hell will mean to a lost soul.

Hell is a realm of conscious existence. Individual souls in hell will know who they are and will be aware of all that is involved in their existence. Their exact status as persons is a question that is open to discussion, for one can hardly be dogmatic in his ideas on the subject. We have an under-standing of the kind of creatures we are in this life, for we are aware of our existence and many of the things that make up our beings. We do not know how much of this will carry over into existence in hell for the lost. It has been suggested that the second death mentioned in Revelation 20:6 is the death of man's spirit.

Men as we know ourselves to be in this life, have several facets or functions of persons: we have a body, we are souls, and we have spirits. There are different interpretations of these ideas, but it seems certain that our spirits constitute that part of our persons that can be made alive in Christ and partake of eternal life. If the spirit dies in the second death, then the person would become a creature without any potential for God, a totally "soulical" creature, bereft of all possibility for good. So the essence of existence for lost souls in eternity will constitute a hell within the person, even though there should be nothing more connected with it. To become this kind of creature is the basest possibility for a human being; he will be given over entirely to his most selfish qualities wherein there is no regard for any other creature in existence. He will be grasping, greedy, avaricious, and ravenous throughout his being, and he will have no interest in the welfare of any other.

Existence anywhere for a creature who is bereft of all good would be intolerable in our way of thinking; however, this is not all that hell will be. Hell itself, as a place of existence, will also be unbearable. One might well refer to the lost soul's existence in hell as an eternity of utter misery-misery that is produced both by what he has become and also by the nature of hell itself. Hell will be a place of utter misery in part because it will be characterized by everything that produces misery in conscious creatures. We may be sure that the things that make men miserable on earth will also make them miserable in hell.

Man's biggest problem on earth is himself; in hell when self will have become totally diabolical, existence will be total misery. Man's second great problem on earth is other people who contest his desires and interfere with his selfish existence. In a state where one's own diabolical self renders him miserable, the presence of vast throngs of creatures of the same kind so closely associated with him that he can never find a moment of reprieve from their presence will make existence all the more a miserable one. Hell is a place that has been prepared for the devil and his kind, and his kind will make existence in their presence more intolerable than the human mind can conceive now.

One of the most galling things possible for a human being on earth is to be forced to exist and work under the tyrannical dictatorship of a person whom he hates, and to do it without any hope for relief or possibility for retaliation. Every creature in hell will be dominated by the fiendish whims of Satan. He will have no recourse but to submit to agonizing slavery. On earth he was promised freedom to do his own thing; he rejected God's loving rule in his heart; now in hell he has become the eternal victim of unbearable dictatorship. There is no freedom in hell.

There is another factor in human existence that produces a miserable condition; it is a total lack of worthwhileness, a deep sense of failure, with no satisfaction derived from the accomplishment and commendation. It is this state of mind that often leads to suicide among men on earth; in hell it will be known in its most intense degree, and there will be no possibility of escape through suicide and no hope for improvement in this meaningless existence. Life on earth is made brighter by one word of praise, appreciation, or commendation. There is a deep sense of satisfaction derived from a hard task well done, a finished product of which a person can be justly proud, or a realization that a worthy contribution has been made. Existence in hell will be an eternity of utter misery partly because of its total futility.

Human misery is also a result of intense cravings that cannot be satisfied. These desires can be developed on earth by cultivating them and seeking to provide what they demand. By the time a person dies, he can have become a victim of numberless burning passions that must be reckoned with if unbearable misery is to be avoided. In hell these desires and passions will have reached their greatest intensity, but there will not be any possible way to alleviate them to any degree. The person who has craved praise will find nothing but blame. The person who has become extremely proud will be buried under shame. The person who has been elated over his intellectual acumen will be but the scum of ignorance and stupidity in hell. The person who has basked in the limelight of worldly popularity on earth will be at the bottom of the pits of nonentity in hell. The demands of self that have enslaved a person on earth will be even more intense in hell, yet total self-crucifixion will be forced upon all creatures there. The misery produced in a person by the conflict between desire and utter inability for satisfaction in hell is too great for us to comprehend fully in this life.

We might seek to catalogue all the words that can be used to express a miserable existence and still fall short of adequately describing the misery of a soul in hell. Loneliness, desolateness, meaninglessness, hopelessness, only begin to describe it. Remorse, regret, self-condemnation, will constantly torment the conscience. Envy, jealousy, malice, ill will, hostility, hatred, will all add to the misery of existence in hell.

One might ask if all souls in hell will experience the same degree of misery. We have already noted that there will be different degrees of intensity in hell for different souls as stated by Jesus in his speaking of some being beaten with few stripes while others were beaten with many stripes. Perhaps the difference will lie in this area of the degree of misery a soul will experience in hell. Jesus indicates that the factor that will determine the degree—few or many stripes—is whether a person disobeys willfully or in ignorance. In other words, sin against light is more severe in its consequence than sin in ignorance of what is right. Ignorance does not remove responsibility for wrongdoing, but it does affect the degree of the penalty for wrongdoing. So we can say that the degree of each person's misery in hell will result from the degree of light he had and rejected in refusing God.

There is another reason we can safely assume that hell will be a place of eternal misery. Not only will everything that is capable of causing a soul to be miserable be there in abundance, but it is also true that there will be nothing there that can prevent or even alleviate utter misery. A person can endure misery for a short time, especially if he knows that relief will come; sometimes pain can be lessened by some form of counter-irritant, or by something that can take a person's mind from his suffering, such as music, or his becoming engrossed in some form of entertainment. At other times a person may be enabled to endure agony simply because of his hope for the future, or because some one dear to him is with him in his suffering. Hell will be a place of utter misery because there will be no relief, no lessening, no distraction, and no hope of any improvement for eternity. The things that cause misery will be eternally set and there will be no escape from them.

In hell there will be no love, for all creatures there will be incapable of loving. There will be no encouragement nor any word of cheer. There will be no forgiveness nor any cleansing from guilt. There will be no kindness, sympathy, or understanding from any creature there. Every creature in hell will have become so totally obsessed with self that concern for any other to any degree will be impossible. Each person there will be completely absorbed by his own misery, and the old adage that "misery loves company" will have been changed to "misery hates company."

It is not difficult for us even now to realize how the trait of selfishness works in a person to produce unbearable existence. A person can grow up as a child wholly wrapped up in his own desires, interests, and satisfactions. His every thought is of himself; he learns to maneuver situations so as to get his way; he manipulates people into centering their attention upon him. Gradually he becomes more and more a self-centered person. He is not interested in anything or anybody except as he himself might through that interest be benefitted. Everything he does has an ulterior motive, which is personal profit in some way. His thoughts are constantly centered upon his own comforts, his efforts are expended to acquire his own desires, his money is spent for selfish satisfactions. He comes to feel that the entire world must revolve around him as a person, and anything that does not recognize him as its center becomes a thorn in his flesh. He is miserable if he cannot have every whim satisfied. He cannot bear to accept or experience anything that is unpleasant for him.

It is not strange that a self-centered person finds life more and more an unbearable existence. He is so tightly wrapped up in himself that what he is in himself and the nature of the world in which he lives contribute to increasing misery. He cannot be happy alone, for the kind of person he has become forbids it. He cannot be happy with others, for they will not fit into his selfish demands. More and more he is forced to be alone, and more and more he becomes more miserable because being alone becomes intolerable. This can actually happen to a person while he is alive in this world. Hell will be much more of the same.

During a person's life on earth he may be able temporarily to escape the realities of a miserable existence by becoming absorbed in some form of pastime such as recreation or music. There will be no music or recreation in hell. On earth a person may deaden his sensitivity to his problems through the use of alcohol or some kind of narcotic; in hell there will be no way of escape from the full fury of soul anguish. On earth men stoically set their wills and take their stand to endure all that life can bring upon them, deriving a sense of conquest in the effort; in hell they will collapse like a weakling with no heart either to fight back or to stand.

No potential for good, no influences toward good, no incentives to be or to do good, will characterize any creature in hell. Total evil without relief or hope of change for eternity will produce a condition of utter misery, and hell can be nothing less than this; in all likelihood, it is far more than the human mind can imagine or human words can express.

With just a meager concept of what hell will be, we can understand why God has done so much for man's redemption, and why He does all that can be done to constrain man to turn from his unbelief and rebellion and come to accept his love, mercy, and grace. God's first desire for every human soul is that he turn from self and receive eternal life through what he himself has done for man. Hell is the only possible place of existence for a soul that has rejected God's offer of eternal life. God has no other alternative.

God's Final Equipping Us for Heaven

*W*e have discussed many aspects of the existence of human souls after death and have suggested certain qualities we believe to be true in heaven and existence in hell. Reference has been made to the belief that the condition of a person in heaven between death and the resurrection of the body is different in some ways from what it will be after the resurrection. This brings up the matter of the resurrection of the body and what that change will mean to the person in heaven. Although we do not know a great deal about the details of the condition of the soul in heaven before the resurrection, we do know the Bible definitely teaches there is to be a resurrection of the body, and we have some ideas concerning what the resurrection body will be.

We derive our hope of the resurrection from the many statements in the New Testament that teach it and also from the fact that Jesus Christ arose from the dead. We shall consider many of the teachings of the New Testament as we seek some answers to our questions on the resurrection. We accept as a well-established fact that Jesus Christ was raised from the dead. This means that his physical body disappeared and he was given a new kind of body in his resurrection; the best we can do is to speak of it as the resurrection body. He proved that his body was real in several ways to his apostles, and we accept their witness to this truth.

When we speak of the resurrection of Jesus Christ, we do not intend to say that his physical body was revived and brought back to its former physical state of being alive biologically. We believe that the people Jesus raised from the dead were restored to physical life and continued to live in the same bodies they had before they died. This is not true of Jesus' resurrection. His resurrection was totally different from a resuscitation of the physical body. He was raised with a new kind of body, and as just stated, the best term we can use in speaking of it is simply to call it a resurrection body. We shall say more about the nature of his body when we come to discuss the likeness of our resurrection bodies to his. Our purpose here is to indicate the fact that he was not brought back to the same kind of life and body he had during his earthly existence.

He was the firstfruits of the dead. This means that his resurrection was the first work of its kind that had ever been done by God. It was as truly a new act of creation by the Holy Spirit as any creative work He has ever done. Jesus Christ alive from the dead in this sense is such a stupendous idea that the natural mind of man cannot accept it. However, this is the essence of our Christian faith: Jesus Christ, crucified, buried, risen, and alive forever! Alive, not limited to a physical body, but alive in a resurrection body that was totally different from anything the world had ever known: this is the meaning of Christ's resurrection

The resurrection of Jesus Christ, according to many Christian theologians, is one of the best established claims of the gospel. It is certainly the crux of the gospel of redemption and the core of our Christian hope. We cannot overemphasize the importance of this greatest of all miracles of all time. It established firmly the deity of Jesus of Nazareth (Rom 1:4). It confirmed his atoning death on the cross (Rom 4:25), for otherwise we would have no indication that his death was acceptable with the Father. His resurrection is proof of the completely satisfactory nature of the work he did in the true holy of holies (Heb 10:12-14). The meaning of the rending of the veil of the Temple (Mark 15:38) was explained and verified by the re-appearance of our Great High Priest after the offering of himself for our sin.

The greatest question ever asked by man, "If a man die, does he go on living?" was answered when Jesus arose from the dead, for his resurrection proved for all time that death is not the end of conscious existence for human souls. Paul said that Jesus brought life and immortality to light through the gospel; the gospel of Jesus Christ reaches its highest peak in his resurrection (I Cor. 15:1-3). According to Peter, our having been begotten unto a living hope is the direct result of the resurrection of Jesus Christ (1 Pet 1:3).

The fact that Jesus Christ arose from the dead means that he is alive today, thus the Christian has a living Savior and Lord (Acts 25:19: Rev 1:18; Rom 6:9; 14:9). The fact that he is alive assures the believer of the same life, both now and forever (John 14:19). Christ's resurrection guarantees the resurrection of believers (Rom 8:11). It also authenticates all the teachings of Jesus Christ. He told his followers many times that he would arise from the dead, and he did. Because of this keeping of his word on this most incredible of all his promises, we can know that he will keep every other promise he made.

Among those promises concerning the future was his promise to return to earth in total and final triumph. The risen living Lord of life will come again, fulfilling his promise just as he did when he arose from the dead.

Our Christian hope of the resurrection of our bodies rests on the strongest points of the gospel of Christ, so we have the same faith-assurance Abraham had, "being fully assured that what He had promised, He was able also to perform" (Rom 4:21). We can also join with Paul in saying, "But having the same spirit of faith according to that which is written, I believed, and therefore did I speak; we also believe, and therefore also we speak; knowing that he that raised up the Lord Jesus shall raise up us also with Jesus, and shall present us with you" (2 Cor 4:13-14). With this hope and assurance, however, we do have some questions on the resurrection of our bodies. Let us consider several of these aspects of the resurrection of our bodies.

Our first question is "When will the dead be raised?" For most of us, the New Testament is clear in its answer to this question; however, there are some who disagree as to the time, placing it immediately after death. They claim that Paul assured the Corinthians that the resurrection body awaits the Christian at death in the words, "For we know that if the earthly house of our tabernacle be dissolved, we have a building from God, a house not made with hands, eternal in the heavens" (2 Cor 5:1). They believe that "a building from God" is the resurrection body; therefore, it is in heaven awaiting our entering into it at death. This is certainly a possible meaning of this statement. However, this is not the only interpretation of the verse, and since there are so many other statements that the resurrection of the body will be at the return of Jesus Christ to earth, it seems more reasonable to interpret Paul's statement in 2 Corinthians 5:1 so as not to produce conflicting claims.

"A building from God" does not necessarily speak of our resurrection bodies. It more likely refers to an abiding place in heaven. Jesus assured the apostles, "I go to prepare a place for you," after having said, "In my Father's house are many mansions," or "dwelling places" (John 14:1-2). So what Paul said is this, "We know that if we are called on to vacate our earthly tabernacles-physical bodies, we shall not be left without an abiding place, for we have a home awaiting us in heaven." He did not intend to speak of the resurrection body, but rather a place where we shall dwell until the resurrection of the body. (See author's view on pages 86 and following.)

Other than this possible exception, the references of the New Testament to the time of the resurrection of the body place it at the Second Coming of Jesus Christ. Paul wrote, "But each in his own order: Christ the firstfruits; then they that are Christ's at his coming (1 Cor 15:23). He assured the Thessalonians, "For the Lord himself shall descend from heaven, with a shout, with the voice of the archangel, and with the trump of God: and the dead in Christ shall rise first" (1 Thess 4:16). The same truth was expressed in 1 Corinthians 15:52, "in a moment, in the twinkling of an eye, at the last trump: for the trumpet shall sound, and the dead shall be raised incorruptible." So we conclude that the dead are to be raised when Christ returns to earth. Paul assured the Thessalonians that when Christ does return, just as surely as he died and rose again, God will bring with him those who have died, and will at that time provide them with resurrection bodies.

When we consider the grandeur of the providing of a resurrection body, we are caused to ask: "What power can accomplish this marvelous feat?" We find the answer in

Romans 8:11, "But if the Spirit of him that raised up Jesus from the dead dwelleth in you, he that raised up Christ Jesus from the dead shall also give life to your mortal bodies through his Spirit that dwelleth in you." There are three important facts in this statement. First, the Holy Spirit is the power that raised Jesus Christ from the dead. In at least twenty-five places in the New Testament we are told that God raised Jesus Christ from the dead; this is the only verse that tells us by what power it was done. Paul spoke of the power of the resurrection of Christ in 1 Corinthians 6:14, "God both raised the Lord, and will raise up us through his power." He mentioned it again in Philippians 3:10, "That I may know him, and the power of his resurrection." This power of the resurrection of Jesus is the Holy Spirit himself.

A second truth in Romans 8:11 is that the same Holy Spirit that raised Jesus will provide resurrection bodies for God's children. The third truth in this verse is that the Holy Spirit who will raise us from the dead already dwells in our spirits. Thus we have in us now the very power of God that will raise us from the dead when Christ returns to earth. Paul indicates that our resurrection is as certain as is the fact that Jesus was raised from the dead. Just as surely as we are children of God, we have the Holy Spirit dwelling in us. Just as surely as we have the Holy Spirit dwelling in us, we have the power of Christ's resurrection in us. This means that our resurrection is assured by the omnipotence of God.

With assurance in our hearts of the *fact* of our resurrection, we find ourselves somewhat like the Corinthians whom Paul convinced of this fact: we want to know, "with what manner of body do they come?" (1 Cor 15:35). What will the resurrection body be like? The first thing we note is that our resurrection bodies will be like the resurrection body of Christ. Paul said in I Corinthians 15:49, "And as we have borne the image of the earthy, we shall also bear the image of the heavenly."

"The earthy" is the physical body we now have; it has been derived from the first Adam and is like Adam's body. "The heavenly" is the resurrection body of Jesus. As we now have a body that bears the image of Adam, in the resurrection, we shall have a body that bears the image of Jesus Christ after his resurrection.

The same truth was expressed by Paul when he wrote in 1 Corinthians 15:20,23: "But now hath Christ been raised from the dead, the firstfruits of them that are asleep, . . . But each in his own order: Christ the firstfruits; then they that are Christ's at his coming." The word "firstfruits" carries several shades of meaning; among them is: that which is first of more of the same to come. So Christs' resurrection body was the firstfruits of the resurrection of the children of God; this means that our bodies will be like his. Paul made this clear to the Philippians, "Who shall fashion anew the body of his glory" (Phil 3:21). "The body of his glory" refers to the resurrection body of Christ. That body will serve as a pattern, a model, for the creation of our resurrection bodies; thus, we shall be like him. Paul wrote to the Romans (8:29) that God has foreordained that we be fashioned after the image of his Son. Whatever else we may say about our resurrection bodies, we can depend on this great truth.

"But," someone will ask, "what *kind* of body did Jesus have after he was raised?" Frankly, nobody knows exactly what kind of body Jesus had. Furthermore, if we could know, we could not describe it without using terms that appear to be self-contradictory. Quite often we speak of Jesus' body as being a spiritual body, yet on second thought, we realize that the two words "spiritual" and "body" refer to ideas that exclude one another. The word "body" carries the idea of shape, substance, size, while "spiritual" means strictly non-material. This is what we mean by self-contradictory terms.

There are some aspects of Jesus' body we can be sure about. For one thing, his body was real. If we choose to use the term "spiritual body," we must never do so with the idea that his resurrection body was only an illusion. At the same time, neither are we to conclude that his resurrection body was flesh and blood as it was before his resurrection. It is true that he insisted to his disciples that his body was real, so invited them to touch it. On this occasion he said, "Why are ye troubled? and wherefore do questionings arise in your heart? See my hands and my feet, that it is I myself: handle me and see; for a spirit hath not flesh and bones, as ye behold me having" (Luke 24:38-39).

The account of this event goes on to say that when Jesus had showed them his hands and feet, he ate a piece of broiled fish, evidently a further proof that he was not a specter or a fantasy, as they definitely felt he must be. Some of us conclude from this experience that Jesus' body must have been actually the same kind of flesh and blood it had been before his death. However, we realize that Jesus at the time this event occurred had entered into a new stage of his work. He had died physically and his body had in some way beyond our understanding become a different kind of body.

The point of the encounter with his disciples in the experience above is that he was *real*, not imaginary. He did appear in bodily form, but the purpose was to prove to them that he was truly alive. They saw him and felt him in a body that was adapted to their physical senses. He did not say he was actually flesh and bones. He said, "A spirit does not have flesh and bones *as you see* me having." Thus we say that he adapted himself to their touch and vision by appearing in a form of flesh and bones. We cannot know for sure what the resurrection body of Jesus was, but we are sure of these two things: it was real, and it was not physical.

We conclude that the same things will be true of our resurrection bodies: they will be real and will consist of something other than material elements. Paul distinguished between the natural, or physical, and the spiritual when he wrote, "Howbeit, that is not first which is spiritual, but that which is natural; then that which is spiritual" (1 Cor 15:46). That is, the natural, or physical body, comes first; we have our physical bodies when we are born into this world. Then, after the resurrection, we have our spiritual bodies. The order is clear as to which comes first; however, our emphasis now is on the fact that our resurrection bodies are to be different from the physical bodies we have now.

The best Paul could do was to speak of the resurrection body as spiritual. He explains this further in verse 44 of this same chapter, "It is sown a natural body; it is raised a spiritual body." Again, the big thing is the fact of the difference between the body we have in this world and the resurrection body. He supports the fact that the resurrection body will not consist of material substance in verse 50 in saying, "Now this I say, brethren, that flesh and blood cannot inherit the kingdom of God." Because of this fact, Paul explained, all of God's children who are alive at the return of Christ must be transformed and given a spiritual body. Otherwise, they could not enter into heaven with the saints who are raised from the dead with resurrection bodies.

Perhaps our problem in trying to understand the resurrection body lies in the fact that we think only in terms of the substance of which the body is composed, when this may not be the meaning of the word "spiritual" as Paul used it of the body. Someone has suggested that Paul did not speak of some spiritual "substance" of which the resurrection body will be composed; rather, he said that the resurrection body, whatever its nature, will be the kind of body our redeemed spirits can inhabit for eternity in heaven. "A spiritual body" thus becomes a body suited for spiritual habitation in a spiritual heaven. Paul's explanation that the new growth from a seed that is planted is entirely different from the seed itself should tell us that the resurrection body will be different from anything we can know about our present physical bodies. Thus we simply speak of it as a spiritual or resurrection body.

This is the best we can do in trying to explain the nature of our resurrection bodies. It is enough to cause us to look forward to this aspect of our Christian hope with great expectancy and assurance. Paul expressed this hope well in these words, "For verily in this we groan, longing to be clothed upon with our habitation which is from heaven" (2 Cor. 5:2).

A further question of interest is, "How will this spiritual body be related to our physical bodies?" Paul discussed this question in 1 Corinthians 15:36 ff. Briefly stated, he said that no seed will grow except it first lies in the ground and dies to its old shape and substance. When it does die to its former state, the life in it springs up in a new form, not at all like the seed which was planted. There is a relationship between the seed and the new plant, but it is not a shape or form relation. Even so, the new spiritual body is related with the person who lived in the old body, but the new is altogether different in substance and form.

Just as there are different kinds of flesh in different types of animal life, and there are different glories in different bodies such as sun and stars, so the resurrection body will be different from the physical body. When a person dies physically, the old body is buried in its corrupt state, while the new body is raised in an incorrupt state. Paul spoke here of the difference between the flesh and blood body that is subject to decay, and the resurrection body that will be spiritual and thus it will not be possible for it to die or become corrupt. Thus, the new body will be basically different from the physical body; it will not consist of material substances.

Did not Paul, however, indicate that there is to be some relation between the physical body and the resurrection body? Is there not a relation between the seed that is planted and the new plant that comes from that seed? The answer is that there is a definite relation, but it is a mysterious one. As best we can understand, the relation between the new plant and the seed from which it springs is in the area of plant life itself. The new plant does not consist of the identical material substance that composed the seed; it is however, alive with the same life germ that was in the seed. Whether we are to go this far in seeking an answer to our question cannot be known for sure, but if we are, we would not be justified in concluding more than the idea that what the resurrection body will have in common with the physical body is the spiritual person himself. Paul plainly said of this relation, "It is sown a natural body; it is raised a spiritual body" (1 Cor 15:44).

Just as God gives each seed its own particular kind of body when it sprouts and grows (1 Cor 15:38), so he will give each redeemed spirit its own spiritual body in the resurrection. It is difficult to see how God would need or use the material substance of the physical body in providing a new spiritual body. As man has received his physical body from Adam through natural generation, so he will receive his spiritual body from Jesus Christ through spiritual principles, the meaning of which has not been revealed to man. The only real carry-over from the physical man to the redeemed spirit in the resurrection body will be the person himself.

We have already referred to 1 Corinthians 15:50: "Now this I say, brethren, that flesh and blood cannot inherit the kingdom of God, neither doth corruption inherit incorruption." That is to say, as noted above, the physical body cannot enter into the spiritual place of heaven, nor can it become an incorruptible spiritual body. The spiritual body will be created by Jesus Christ; this creation is the same as the resurrection of the body.

We might wonder what the spiritual body will look like, keeping in mind that we do not speak of "looks" from a physical viewpoint. How will it look from a spiritual viewpoint? It is difficult to find a direct answer to this question in the Bible, so we must rely on deducing our answer from principles given in the Bible. From what has just been said above concerning any carry over from the physical body, we can conclude that the spiritual body will not resemble our earthly body. This means that physical "looks" and physical defects will not be a part of our spiritual bodies. The spiritual body will be created to express perfectly the spiritual person we have become. Thus our spiritual "looks" will reflect exactly what we are from a moral and spiritual viewpoint. The essence of our being, the character of our real selves, will constitute what we look like in our spiritual bodies. Since our spiritual ideal in this life is to become Christlike, and spiritual maturity is measured by our Christlikeness, the beauty of our spiritual bodies will be determined by how much like Jesus Christ we have become in our spiritual growth.

This should not be difficult to understand when we remember that this principle works to a large degree in regard to what we truly are as persons and the way we come to look in our physical bodies. A person's countenance eventually comes to reflect what he is as a person. A sixteen-year-old girl is naturally pretty whether she has a perfectly formed face or not; she has the natural beauty of youth. However, when she is sixteen, she is not to receive credit for her beauty. When she reaches the age of forty, she will deserve either her beauty or her lack of it, as the case may be, for when she is forty, she will have begun to reflect in her face the kind of person she is. True beauty is not just skin deep; it is a reflection of the real person in the countenance.

This principle is also illustrated in the resemblance that develops between husbands and wives. It is often noted that they come to look alike after living together for thirty or forty years. Someone might explain this similarity by saying that they resembled each other when they were married, but it seems more likely that over the years the two have experienced together the same hopes, desires, emotions, successes, and failures that make up life. They have generally reacted similarly to theses experiences and have had produced in them similar qualities of character. As a result, they have come to look alike in their physical facial features. In a more accurate manner, what a person truly is in his spiritual person will determine what he will look like in his spiritual body. It might be in order to observe that a Christian in this life is becoming the kind of person that will determine how he will look in his spiritual body. We shall have more to say on this subject later.

Let us close this section of our discussion by reasserting the idea that the bodies of all believers who die before the return of Jesus Christ to this earth will be raised at his return. This resurrection of the dead will precede the changing of the bodies of those believers who are alive at that time. Thus all of God's children will come to have a resurrection body, a spiritual body that is created for the spirit's existence in heaven. Paul suggested to the Thessalonian Christians that this part of Christian hope should serve as a basis for helpful encouragement when Christians lose loved ones through physical death. After having assured them of the fact that Christ will return, and that when He does, the dead will be raised, he writes, "Wherefore comfort one another with these words" (1 Thess 4:18).

Thus, in the resurrection of all Christians, God will have prepared his children for their eternal relationship with him in heaven. However, there is one more great event we need to consider before feeling we have ended our search concerning our eternal destiny; this is the subject of our next section.

Final Assignment to Eternal Destiny

One of the most awesome ideas in the entire Bible is its teaching that one day after everything having to do with our life on earth has been completely finished, we shall all stand before the God of this universe in judgment. We have already noted that one of our most precious possessions as a human being is our freedom of self-determination, the power to choose for ourselves what we shall become and what we shall do. We have also assured ourselves that with the use of every freedom goes personal responsibility for the way in which it is used. The Bible teaches that quite often we begin reaping in this life what we have sown, but that the final accounting to God will be made in the great day of judgment.

The writers of the New Testament realized that many things in this world are out of balance; many evils go unpunished, and in many cases, justice is not executed. However, they are equally certain that there is a day coming in which all inequities will be righted and all wrongs will be dealt with in justice. It is also clearly indicated in the Bible that at the time of the final judgment, all human creatures will enter into their eternal state, each with his full and just desserts. From there on throughout eternity, it will be perfect heaven for God's children and all hell for those who have rejected God. It is important that we understand some things about this great day, for it looms large on every human horizon.

First, let us clarify some things about God and the judgment. Some people seem to feel that God will take delight in being able to condemn the lost to an eternal hell. They attribute to God a spirit of vindictiveness, in the sense of fighting back or getting even, and indicate that he will take gloating pleasure in the suffering of those who have rejected him. These ideas are derived possibly from statements made about God and the judgment in the New Testament. For instance, Paul says in Romans 1:18, "For the wrath of God is revealed from heaven against all ungodliness and unright-

eousness of men, who hinder the truth in unrighteousness."
He writes in Romans 5:9, "Much more then, being now justified by his blood, shall we be saved from the wrath of God
through him." In addition, Paul quotes Moses: "For it is
written, Vengeance belongeth unto me; I will recompense,
saith the Lord" (Rom 12:19). He also writes, "Who shall suffer
punishment, even eternal destruction from the face of the
Lord and from the glory of his might" (2 Thess 1:9).

Mistaken ideas about God have arisen because these
words are given the same meaning when speaking of him that
they ordinarily carry when applied to men, and this meaning
is then used in defining the judgment. We think of vengeance
as a vindicative "getting even" with some one who has mis-
treated us. However, the word for "vengeance" and the one
for "punishment" are derived from a word that means "to
deal in perfect justice." There is no spirit of vindictiveness
involved in the words. To say that vengeance belongs to God
is to say that only God is capable of dealing in perfect justice
with man. Man is forbidden to exercise vengeance because he
cannot deal in perfect justice and will likely be vindictive in
his treatment of one who has wronged him. God can and will
deal with all men in perfect justice where justice is demanded.

The vengeance of God means that after he has done all he
can to redeem man and man refuses to accept his love and
grace, there is nothing left for him to do except to deal with
that man in perfect justice unmixed with mercy. This he will
do without any spirit of vindictiveness. God will never take
pleasure in dealing in perfect justice with any creature. Peter
writes, "The Lord is not slack concerning his promise, but is
longsuffering to you ward, not wishing that any should
perish, but that all should come to repentance" (2 Pet 3:9). His
longsuffering is not to be misinterpreted as weakness or
indifference to man's sin. Rather, it is evidence of his loving
desire for man to repent and be saved. However, when man
goes on in rebellion and unbelief, there must come a day
when God will deal in perfect justice with him.

The "punishment" which will come to the unrepentant is
of the same nature. It is not at all that God takes delight in

punishing a person. It is rather that when he must finally deal with one in justice, that justice will be such that from the viewpoint of the one who receives it, it will be punishment. He will receive exactly what he deserves, and that will be the natural results of his rebellious ways. These results will be his punishment. It will not be a sadist god gloating over and enjoying the suffering of his victims. Really, it will be a God who has loved and lost in that particular case, and He will have lost only because of the stubborn will of the individual involved.

The term "the wrath of God" has a similar meaning when rightly understood. Man thinks of wrath as of a person who loses himself in a fit of temper and gleefully causes his enemy to suffer. This concept is not only unworthy of God, it is really an insult to him. Paul speaks of the wrath of God in Romans 1:18; Ephesians 5:6 and Colossians 3:6.

There are two ideas contained in the use of the word for wrath. First, it expresses God's natural repugnance toward all evil. Since God is holy, there can be no harmony in his Being with any kind of evil. There is that in him which is directly the opposite of evil. This truth should not be omitted from the meaning of wrath. A second factor in this term as applied to God is that we are not to read into it the same attitudes that we attribute to man in speaking of his wrath. God does not lose himself in a fit of temper with a desire to fight back at man. God does have an abhorrence of all evil, but the exercise of his wrath is a removal of his mercy in dealing with man and a righteous execution of justice without vindictiveness. Paul explains that God's wrath upon man's ungodliness in this life consists primarily in his giving man over to the slavery of his passions wherein he becomes more and more corrupt in mind and character (see Rom. 1:24,26,28).

If this be true concerning the exercise of God's wrath in this life, it will likely be that the execution of God's wrath in the judgment will consist of a righteous and just commitment of the unsaved to the eternal results of sin, which will be utter separation from God. God's wrath is a terrible thing, not because it is a bad quality of an otherwise good God, but rather because it means that eventually God will deal in perfect justice with all men who have rejected His love and mercy. So we are not to feel that at that judgment God will take delight in being able to condemn the lost to an eternal hell, God will not gloat over the fact.

There is another misconception about the judgment that one should avoid; it is that the judgment will be the time and place where destiny will be determined. Some teachers have painted a word picture of the judgment in which all men are lined up at the judgment awaiting their turn to learn where they will spend eternity. The impression is given that this will be a time of uncertainty and tenseness for each one as he draws nearer and nearer to God, wondering whether or not he will be accepted and allowed to enter heaven. We would not take away any of the awesomeness of the judgment for any person, yet this concept of the judgment that a person will not know his eternal destiny until he learns it at that time is not according to truth.

A person's eternal destiny is settled in this life, while he is alive and conscious, capable of determining his personal relationship with God for himself. When physical death comes, there will be no more question about where a person will spend eternity, for it will have already been settled. Any hope for an opportunity after death to change a person's decision that has been made in this life is a hope without scriptural foundation. It is also unscriptural to suggest that a person will be uncertain as to his eternal destiny during the period between his physical death and the judgment. When a human being dies, he knows immediately *where* he will spend eternity.

Someone may argue against this idea and cite the teachings of Jesus in Matthew 25:31 ff. to support his claim. In this passage Jesus spoke of the time when the Son shall sit on the throne of his glory and all the nations will be gathered before him. At that time, he shall separate the people as a shepherd separates the sheep from the goats, and shall then deal with each group in judgment. From a casual reading of this account and by interpreting it according to our material world, one might well conclude that the distinctions and separation will not occur until the day of judgment. He might go on to conclude that all nations of people, that is, all the human beings who have ever lived, will come to that time to find out where they will spend eternity, and that they will not know until they are told to go either with the sheep or with the goats. However, a more careful reading will harmonize this passage with other clear teachings that the judgment will not be the time and place where destiny is determined.

First, we must realize that the judgment will not take place until the material universe has ceased to exist. The "Day of the Lord" was used as another way of referring to the day of judgment. Peter wrote that the "day of the Lord will come as a thief; in which the heaven shall pass away with a great noise, and the elements shall be dissolved with fervent heat, and the earth and the works that are therein shall be burned up" (2 Pet 3:10). This means that the scene described by Jesus in Matthew 25 is to take place when time has ceased to be and where space does not exist. Therefore, we are not to understand the occasion as though Jesus were sitting on a throne in space and people of all nations were gathered in one place to be divided as sheep and goats.

There is no way we can visualize that great day of judgment, for it will take place under conditions that are entirely new. Jesus resorted to language of men in speaking of it, but we are not to interpret the language in such a way as to construct doctrines that are contrary to the rest of scriptural teaching on the subject. There will be a great day of judgment; all human beings will be there to be judged in righteous judgment; however, the scene painted in human terms is not to be interpreted as taking place in this world of time and space.

On the positive side, several great truths stand out in the judgment scene Jesus gave. The fact of the judgment is definitely settled. The universality of the judgment is equally clear; this is the meaning of the term "all the nations." The truth is evident that there are not many different groups of people in their relationship with God; there are only two. Men are either right with God or they are wrong with him-either sheep or goats. There is no "neutral corner," nor is there to be an "in-between place" where men spend eternity. Then it is plainly indicated that God will deal with people individually; although each person will be a part of his own particular group, he will be in that group because of his personal relationship with God on earth.

A final truth in this depicted scene is that the life and works of the individual will enter into this final accounting before God. We must not conclude that the individual is placed in the group as a sheep or a goat because of his "doing it unto one of the least of these." That separation is determined by something else. The teaching here concerning good works is to be harmonized with the truths we have noted on the subject of rewards for service. The different ones are to be separated into groups and then they are rewarded because of their faithful service rendered to needy people on earth.

Thus we see that the teachings of Jesus in this great passage on the judgment do not conflict with our statement that the purpose of the judgment is not to determine eternal destiny for people. The one thing that will determine the eternal destiny of a human soul at the judgment will already have been settled before physical death.

The parable of the marriage feast in which the distinguishing mark of the invited guests was the wedding garment indicates that the one thing that will determine a person's status before God is whether he has the righteousness of Jesus Christ before he enters God's presence. As we have clearly shown, this is determined by each individual soul before his death on earth. In spite of all the natural desires of mankind to the contrary, there is no clear scriptural basis for a hope of a second chance after physical death.

If the judgment will not be a time when a person's eternal place of destiny is determined, what will be its purpose? Why have a judgment at all if eternal destinies have already been settled? First, it will be a time of full revelation of truth to all creatures. The devil has been busy for eons of time deceiving men with his cunning lies. There is no area of truth that he has not invaded and perverted. Every human being who rejects God and His truth has been convinced by Satan's lies to do so; he lives and dies in spiritual darkness, never having seen the light. Even the believer who has accepted God's revelation of himself has at best only a partial understanding of truth. The full import of what the Christian does know cannot be realized in this life. So both the saved and the unsaved are in need of full revelation of truth.

The Bible speaks clearly on this idea. Paul wrote, "But after thy hardness and impenitent heart treasurest up for thyself wrath in the day of wrath and revelation of the righteous judgment of God" (Rom 2:5). Paul wrote in 2 Corinthians 5:10, "For we must all be made manifest before the judgment seat of Christ; that each one may receive the things done in the body, according to what he hath done, whether it be good or bad."

It seems certain that Jesus is speaking of the judgment in saying, "Fear them not therefore: for there is nothing covered, that shall not be revealed; and hid, that shall not be known" (Matt 10:26). Paul applied this idea of revelation to the quality of Christian life and service in 1 Corinthians 3:12-13: "But if any man buildeth on the foundation gold, silver, costly stones, wood, hay, stubble; each man's work shall be made manifest; for the day shall declare it, because it is revealed in fire; and the fire itself shall prove each man's work of what sort it is."

We might suggest that this final and full revelation for the redeemed will consist of having God's truth made clear to them. God himself will be understood as fully as it is possible for a creature to understand the Creator. The full meaning of sin, of unbelief, of rejected love, will be realized; this will at the same time give deeper meaning to God's mercy, love and grace. Thus redemption will come to be understood in its eternal significance, and the redeemed of all ages will join angelic voices in ascribing praise to Jesus Christ, "Worthy is the Lamb that hath been slain to receive the power, and riches, and wisdom, and might, and honor, and glory, and blessing" (Rev 5:12). There will be no questions left unanswered; there will be no cause for any doubts, "For now we see in a mirror, darkly; but then face to face: now I know in part; but then shall I know fully even as also I was fully known (1 Cor 13:12). Satanic deceit will have ceased; physical limitation will no longer exist; prejudices will no longer interfere with the truth. At the same time, God will have clearly revealed the mysteries that could not be made known to men during their life on earth. So the judgment day will be a time when full revelation is made to God's children.

The judgment for the lost will also be a time of revelation of truth. Minds that were totally blinded by Satan on earth to the gospel of Jesus Christ will be enlightened to understand and enabled to realize the truth and significance of God's love. They will come to know that their status in eternity has resulted from their own choices; they will recognize the enormity of their mistake, yet they will have no basis for blaming God for their predicament. They will fully understand what eternity holds for them, and at the time be keenly aware of what heaven could have meant to them. They will wonder how it was possible for them to have been so foolish as to close their hearts to God's overtures of love and duped into falling for Satan's lies. So the judgment will be a time for the full revelation of truth to all creatures. This in itself will hold great importance in the meaning of eternal destiny for all, both the saved and the lost.

There is another meaningful purpose in the judgment: it will be the time when each person will give an account of his life on earth and will receive from God what his life and works have merited. Jesus said, "For the Son of man shall come in the glory of his Father with his angels; and then shall he render unto every man according to his deeds" (Matt 16:27). Paul wrote in Romans 2:4 ff. "Or despisest thou the riches of his goodness and forbearance and longsuffering, not knowing that the goodness of God leadeth thee to repentance? but after thy hardness and impenitent heart treasurest up for thyself wrath in the day of wrath and revelation of the righteous judgment of God; who will render to every man according to his works: to them that by patience in well-doing seek for glory and honor and incorruption, eternal life: but unto them that are factious, and obey not the truth, but obey unrighteousness, shall be wrath and indignation, tribulation and anguish, upon every soul of man that worketh evil." Paul's statement in 2 Corinthians 5:10 is equally clear, "For we must all be made manifest before the judgment-seat of Christ; that each one may receive the things done in the body, according to what he has done, whether it be good or bad." The same writer said, "so then each one of us shall give account of himself to God" (Rom 14:12).

There are two things emphasized in these statements: Each individual will give an account to God, and each one will receive according to what he has done on earth. The idea in giving an account to God seems to be that each individual will answer to God for himself, he will be allowed to speak for himself; thus, the judgment is to be universal and at the same time personal. This direct and personal accounting to God will be followed by God's dealing with each one according to his stewardship accounting; this means that God will render to each person according to his works. We must remember as noted above that eternal destiny is not the question to be settled here. Each person will know before the judgment where he will spend eternity, so this rendering to each one will have to do with something other than where a person will go after the judgment.

For the lost soul the judgment will be the time when all the results of his choices will be placed upon him. The influences of his life and works will have been building up for years or ages since his life on earth, and at the judgment his investment with interest will be returned to him. This indicates that there will be differences in lost souls in eternity. All will be in hell, but lost souls will not all experience the same intensity of hell, for God will "render to every man according to his deeds."

Jesus states this in Luke 12:47-48, "And that servant, who knew his lord's will, and made not ready, nor did according to his will, shall be beaten with many stripes; but he that knew not, and did things worthy of stripes, shall be beaten with few stripes." There is no reliable way by which we can know what Jesus meant by the words "few" and "many" stripes, but it does denote some kind of difference in what hell will mean to different people. Our purpose at present it to understand that whatever differences there will be in the status of the lost in eternity, the judgment is the time and place when those differences will be realized and received by each one.

For the Christian, the judgment will be the time when rewards for Christian service are received. We have already discussed this subject and need only to note here that the bestowing of rewards will take place at the judgment. This is the meaning of phrases like, "that each one may receive the things done in the body." The commendation of the faithful servant, "Well done, good and faithful servant: thou hast been faithful over a few things, I will set thee over many things: enter thou into the joy of thy Lord," will evidently be spoken at the judgment. From there on throughout the unfolding of eternity, God's children will share in the glories of heaven while centering their own existence upon glorifying the eternal God whose love made it all a reality.

There is one further word that needs to be said concerning the *time* of the judgment. We have already said that time as we know it now will have ceased, so the "time" we speak of simply relates the judgment with the other events that are to come about. Scofield's system of scheduling events assures us that there are to be three separate judgments. According to this system, the redeemed are to be judged immediately following the rapture. Then there is to be a judgment when Christ sets up his millennial kingdom in Jerusalem. Finally, the great white throne judgment is to follow the millennium at which time the wicked dead are to be judged.

When we study the Bible without the predetermined program as a guide, we find an entirely different concept. The judgement is always presented in the Bible as one great event and no suggestion is made of more than one. There is not one time when the judgment is referred to as the *days* of judgment; it is always as Paul stated it, "God has appointed *a day* in which he will judge the world in righteousness" (Acts 17:31).

Jesus made it even narrower as to time when he said, "Marvel not at this: for the hour cometh in which all that are in the tombs shall hear his voice, and shall come forth; they that have done good unto the resurrection of life; and they that have done evil, unto the resurrection of judgment" (John 5:28-29). "The hour" could hardly mean other than a set time at which both the righteous and the unrighteous are raised and judged. We should remember also that in the scene in Matthew 25:31 ff., we have seen that both the sheep and the goats are present at the same place and time and for the same purpose: both are judged, as that word applies to each, the saved and the lost.

The time of the final judgment will be following the return of Jesus Christ; the material universe will have come to an end; the dead, both righteous and unrighteous, will have been raised; and all accountable creatures to be judged will have been gathered unto judgment. From this point on, we do not need to concern ourselves with time. It is needless to reason as to how long the judgment will last, for when this material universe has ceased to exist, there will no longer be what we now know as time.

References in the Bible to the matter of how the different events connected with this period are related are inconclusive. We shall do well to be satisfied with what we can know without demanding a detailed program of the events that God has set within his own authority. Jesus' words to the apostles at the time of his ascension apply to the judgment also, "It is not for you to know times or seasons" (Acts 1:7). What we can know are those ideas we have presented in this section of our study.

Getting Ready for Heaven

$\mathcal{M}$ ost people who are able to derive the greatest good from a great event give much time to the matter of preparation. Since heaven is the greatest of all future events for a human soul, it is only right that we exercise the highest wisdom in preparing for it. We are not surprised to learn that Jesus urged this very thing upon all men. In the parable of the ten virgins (Matt 25:1-13), Jesus strongly stressed the matter of preparation for his return and all that is connected with it.

Several suggestions are given in the parable concerning this preparation. It must be right and adequate. The main point of the parable is that a person cannot afford to be mistaken, for when the time comes, it is too late to make changes. It is also clear that the time to make this preparation is now; postponement is dangerous, and as in the case of the foolish virgins, may be fatal.

Preparation for a vital matter such as our eternal destiny must not be delayed one moment. Then, having made the preparation that can and must be made now, it is also important that our preparation be of such nature that we are ready at all times for the great event to occur. This was the climax of the parable; Jesus closed it with the admonition, "Watch therefore, for ye know not the day nor the hour." It is only under these conditions of right and ready preparation that a Christian can joyously look forward to that great day.

In the light of these truths, our question immediately becomes: "What preparation is right and adequate?" For our answer, let us recall the things we said will determine our status in heaven and go on to see what we can do about them now.

The first things we mentioned is the matter of being made spiritually alive. We have said that heaven is a place of spiritual life and that only those who have been made alive with the life of God can enter into heaven when they die. This being true, there is nothing in all the realm of possibilities for a human soul that is as important as our partaking of eternal

life while we are living in this world. It were better that we
had never been born than to live our life without being born
again.

Nonexistence would be a thousand times better than any
existence without God and the life that only he can provide.
There cannot possibly be any profit in obtaining the whole
world if in doing so, we fail to obtain eternal life. There cannot be any true loss if it is sustained in obtaining true life, for
in partaking of the Life of God, we receive that which is more
valuable than all else.

Thus every human soul should give priority to becoming
rightly related with God. It is vain to think of anything else
that has to do with heaven until we have come into a direct,
personal, living, spiritual relationship with the Living God.
This is our first need and it is possible for all who will yield
heart and life to God as Savior and Lord. Once you have confronted God in Jesus Christ, have seen and felt your need,
have yielded yourself to God as your God, and have invited
him into your life, you are made a new creation in Christ
Jesus and have the life of God that fits you for entrance into
heaven when you die. In speaking of preparation for heaven,
this is not an option; it is a must.

The second thing that will affect our status in heaven is
our spiritual growth and maturity. We have noted that the
time for our growth is during our life on earth; whether we
shall continue to grow in heaven cannot be settled for sure,
but it is pretty certain that what we become in this life definitely affects what we shall be in heaven. So when we think
about getting reading for heaven, we should consider the
entire matter of our growth in the grace and knowledge of
Jesus Christ.

This is not to be a selfish desire for personal gain, for our
desire to become more Christlike is not real if it is self-centered. Becoming like Christ is coming more and more to seek
only the glory of the Father, and our desire to grow in grace
and knowledge is with the same high purpose in mind. The
greater our spiritual stature, whatever that will mean, the
greater our ability to glorify God in heaven. Because of this,

we are exhorted again and again in the New Testament to care for our spiritual growth.

Let us mention a few of these exhortations. The verse leading up to Peter's "But grow in the grace and knowledge of our Lord and Saviour Jesus Christ" is this: "Wherefore, beloved, seeing that ye look for these things, give diligence that ye may be found in peace, without spot and blameless in his sight" (2 Pet 3;14). John commented concerning the fact that one day we shall be like Christ, "And every one that hath this hope set on him purifieth himself, even as he is pure" (1 John 3:3). Paul wrote to the Corinthians, "Having therefore these promises, beloved, let us cleanse ourselves from all defilement of flesh and spirit, perfecting holiness in the fear of God" (2 Cor 7:1). In the light of the fact that Christians will one day be manifested in glory with Christ, Paul urged the Colossians to put to death the sins of the flesh and to cultivate qualities of spiritual maturity (Col 3:5 ff.). In a true sense, practically every admonition to Christians in the New Testament is connected with the broader meaning of spiritual growth.

We have noted that every soul born of the Spirit of God is capable of growth; at the same time, we said that this growth is not automatic; rather, it depends on our own responses to God and our care for our relationship with him. Thus this matter of getting ready for heaven is to begin when we are saved and is to continue just as long as we are allowed to live in this world. Life itself is truly a time and place for preparation for heaven. Knowing *what* we are to do in this aspect of preparation, our next move is to discover *how* we are to do this.

We are told that we are to grow in the grace and knowledge of Jesus Christ. When we grow *in* grace and knowledge, we also grow in spiritual stature through this grace and knowledge. God's grace and knowledge are means of growth as well as being areas of growth. So our first step in spiritual growth is to open our hearts and lives to God's grace and to search diligently for a deeper and clearer understanding of what God has revealed through Jesus Christ.

In what way do we grow in God's grace? This calls for a definition of that grace. God's grace is clearly God's love in action on our behalf; God's love is his self-giving in bringing his children into their highest possibility. Thus, our growth in God's grace, at least in part, is our partaking of God's abundant provisions for our spiritual best interests. To be sure, the greatest need every Christian has is for a more perfect relationship with God, so we grow in God's grace as we open our hearts and lives for the filling of the Holy Spirit, for he is our helper in growth as well as in every other area of need.

We do not need to explain how we are to grow in the knowledge of Jesus Christ. We do need to say that the "knowledge" Peter spoke of is not just an intellectual acquaintance with the historical facts concerning Jesus' life and works, nor is it a theoretical understanding of even the great doctrines of the Bible. The knowledge that produces spiritual growth is a spiritual understanding and acceptance of the truth of God as revealed in the person of Jesus Christ. The growth results from the experience of this truth, just as physical growth comes from the assimilation of the food we eat. The importance of the Bread of life in spiritual growth can hardly be overemphasized.

In the light of these things, it is not at all strange that Peter would close his Second Epistle with this admonition to grow in the grace and knowledge of Jesus Christ. He has begun the epistle (1:2) with the prayer, "Grace to you and peace be multiplied in the knowledge of God and of Jesus our Lord." That is, grace and peace are multiplied in the believer's heart and life as he comes to a fuller experiential understanding of God as he is manifested in Jesus Christ. He goes on to explain this provision by saying, "Seeing that his divine power hath granted unto us all things that pertain unto life and godliness, through the knowledge of him that called us by his own glory and virtue" (1:3). Spiritual growth has been made possible in every area and to its highest degree for all of God's children in "all things that pertain unto life and godliness." There is no need for which God has not amply provided. It is known by the individual "through the knowledge of him that called us." Thus a growth in the knowledge of Jesus Christ is basic in spiritual maturity.

That this is not merely an intellectual understanding of facts is indicated by Peter's insistence that what is learned of Jesus Christ in the form of knowledge must be translated into character and life. In 1:5 he says, "Yea, and for this very cause adding on your part all diligence, in your faith supply virtue; and in your virtue knowledge."

"For this very cause" refers to the fact that God has made ample provision for every need of the believer. The inference is that since this is true, each person is to give himself in all earnestness to appropriating what God has made available. It is absolutely necessary that each individual "supply" what God has provided. This word means to partake of lavishly.

God's provision is in abundance, and the partaking should also be in abundance. Just as a person will not derive physical sustenance from food that he does not eat, likewise neither can he profit from even the richest of God's provisions except as he partakes of them. When a person fails to partake of that which makes for spiritual growth, he simply remains a spiritual baby and fails to mature as he should. On the other hand, when he does avail himself of what God has provided, he becomes more and more a spiritually mature person.

Peter said, "For if these things are yours and abound, they make you to be not idle nor unfruitful unto the knowledge of our Lord Jesus Christ" (1:8). He closed this great section of teaching on spiritual growth with the words, "Wherefore, brethren, give the more diligence to make your calling and election sure; for if ye do these things, ye shall never stumble; for thus shall be richly supplied unto you the entrance into the eternal kingdom of our Lord and Savior Jesus Christ (1:10-11).

Our entire idea that spiritual growth on earth will affect our status in heaven is strongly suggested in this passage. Our maturity definitely makes a difference while we are in the body. Peter said that those who fail to grow are like a near-sighted person trying to distinguish some distant object: he "squints" his eyes. This is the meaning of the word translated "blind" in verse 9. Spiritually immature Christians are not prudent in being able to distinguish between good and evil, or between the good, better, and best. Spiritual growth enables a Christian to be wise in recognizing the truth about practical matters in life.

It is also true that our spiritual growth affects our status in heaven and should be carefully and diligently cared for. Peter said, "For thus shall be richly supplied unto you the entrance into the eternal kingdom of our Lord and Saviour Jesus Christ." His "for thus" refers to "if ye do these things"; this in turn, refers to the entire truth given in verses 5-10. The substance of the entire passage (1:2-11) is that God has made ample provision for every need his children have in this life in order for them to grow spiritually. That being true, each one of us must see to it that we avail ourselves of his provisions. We are to partake lavishly and diligently, for the manner in which we finally enter into heaven is determined by this very thing. As God has *richly* provided (vv. 3-4), and as we *lavishly* partake of His provisions and thereby become mature and fruitful "branches on the Vine," we shall be *richly* supplied in our entrance into heaven.

We do not understand all that is involved in the differences, but we do know that entrance into heaven will be different for Christian people. Some of us will get there "by the skin of our teeth." That means that we are saved, we partake of spiritual life, but we do not grow in God's grace, so come to the end of life spiritually immature, and we enter into heaven in that condition. On the other hand, when we do grow in God's grace and knowledge, when "we do these things" of this passage, then we shall come to the end of this life and be given a rich entrance into heaven. We shall not need to be dragged into port by a tug boat, but having completed our life journey, we shall sail into port with everything in shipshape condition, rejoicing in the victory that is ours and manifesting to the full our triumph in Jesus Christ.

We cannot give further time to this vitally important item in getting ready for heaven except to note that Peter used the term "all diligence" in speaking of the manner in which we are to do it. This word was used in speaking of a successful businessman and the application of his whole person in becoming successful. Even so, we should apply ourselves *diligently* in this matter of spiritual growth.

The third thing we said will affect our status in heaven will be the rewards we receive for earthly service. Two things were said about rewards that should be considered in getting ready for heaven. First, we said that we shall be rewarded on the basis of our faithfulness in both our abilities and in our opportunities to use our abilities. We can derive satisfaction in knowing that God will not judge and reward us on the basis of what some other person has or does; he will consider our own faithfulness. Furthermore, we can know that we can be as faithful in what we have and can do as any other person. Realizing these things, our preparation for heaven must consist in part in seeking to be as faithful as we can at all times. Our faithfulness is to be always in our relationship with God. Oftentimes, people will put pressure on us to give our time and abilities as they dictate, but our faithfulness must be to God. We alone are responsible for determining this matter.

We love people; we serve God through ministering to others; yet, at the same time, our first loyalty is to him. Whatever is involved, if we would be ready for heaven, we must be "faithful unto death." This means that we maintain our faithfulness to God even if we must die in order to do it.

Very few things bring so great glory to God as the faithfulness of his children. Peter said that the purified faith of God's children that results from trials and testings is precious because it will "be found unto praise and glory and honor at the revelation of Jesus Christ" (1 Pet 1:7). So let us be faithful at all costs.

The other thing that determines our rewards in heaven is the *kind* of service we render. You will recall the "wood, hay, and stubble" service that is burned, as well and the "gold, silver and precious stone" service that will be rewarded. You will also remember that we mentioned three things that make the difference. Our motive must be love; our purpose must be the glory of God; and our service must be wrought in the

Spirit of God. Our preparation for heaven includes an understanding of these things and constant care in seeing that our
service measures up to these standards.

We need to search our motives for doing what we do and
pray for God's grace to serve Him and our fellowman in love.
We need to crucify the old man and refuse to seek selfish
ends through our good deeds, keeping in mind that the glory
of God is the only worthy purpose for true service. In order
to do this, we need to read frequently passages like Matthew
6:1-18, along with statements like 1 Corinthians 10:31, "Therefore, whether ye eat or drink, or whatever ye do, do all to the
glory of God."

Similar admonitions are given in Colossians 3:17 and 1
Peter 4:11. It is not enough that we know these things: we
must keep them constantly before us, or we shall find ourselves drifting into worldly ways and seeking selfish glory. If
we do this in the right spirit, we shall not become so self-
critical that we cripple ourselves.

Perhaps our most difficult problem in Christian service is
to maintain a relationship with God in which what we do is
truly his working in and through us. Our preparation in this
area should consist of a realization of the truths we suggested
in discussing this point earlier. Let us know that "it is God
who worketh in you both to will and to work, for his good
pleasure." Knowing that God is in us and he will work
through us, let us do what we know to do, fully assured that
God is working through us. We do not depend on ourselves,
we depend on God. We look to him to take what we do and
accomplish his work. This kind of service removes a great
deal of the stress we usually feel, and at the same time, it is
the wisest kind of preparation we can make for the time when
God will work in and through us perfectly in heaven.

In a very true sense, we are learning now how to be used
of God when we get to heaven; let us learn well, knowing that
God will use us in heaven to the fullest degree we are capable
of being used. Think of the glory of this possibility and you
will come to a stronger conviction of its weighty significance.
Get ready for heaven! Do it by learning well how to be used

of God. It is not enough simply to become a Christian. Although becoming a Christian is absolutely essential, there is far mare to this matter than being saved. There is an eternity that is ours when we are saved, and that eternity will not consist of empty idleness where we swing in a hammock sipping pink lemonade. God will use us forever; and we are determining now, during this life, how fully and effectively He will be able to use us. He has made ample provision for us in this training camp; we must not be dilatory, negligent, or presumptuous. We do not wonder at Paul's urgent word, "And this, knowing the season, that it is time for you to awake out of sleep: for now is salvation nearer to us than when we first believed" (Rom 13:11).

There is one further word I would say on this matter of getting ready for heaven. Having heeded the advice above, we need to develop a Christian attitude toward life, death, and eternity. I say develop, for we do not have it naturally, and we shall find that it is not overly simple to develop. We shall likely not be able to overcome completely our natural inclination to draw back from physical death. We *can* bring ourselves to consider death in the light of our faith and thereby condition ourselves to be prepared to face it when it comes. This does not mean that we keep our minds under the shadow of death in an effort to conquer our natural fears. It does mean that we become convinced of the truth of God's revelation and that we develop our attitudes toward death in the light of that truth.

There is one practical suggestion I am reluctant to make because it lends itself to misunderstanding. We should practice dying. Again, let me insist this does not mean we should envelop ourselves in a dark cloud of foreboding, nor should we need often to do anything of this sort.

I believe we could rationally and unemotionally think through the experience of death. How are we to think at that time? How can we apply our faith so as to derive the greatest help and support in that hour? What promise of God could mean most to us when we realize that in a few minutes we shall be in His presence? This is the kind of "practicing" I refer to, and it can bring rich dividends to our hearts when that inevitable hour strikes. It is not wise to make preparation for every other experience we think may lie ahead, and totally ignore this one thing that we know we must face.

I am aware that regardless of what we may do in an effort to prepare, the real thing will be different from a projected idea; yet, at the same time, this is a reasonable part of heeding Jesus' word, "Therefore, be ye also ready." Get ready for heaven now.

From Here on in through Hope

*T*o this position we have come; in these convictions we stand; and from this point on we move in an ever brighter hope. It is this hope we want to consider now, realizing that understanding our hope is a vital part of our preparation for the future. Most of us likely have not taken time to analyze our hope; as a result of this failure, we do not understand or treasure that hope as we should. We have only to consider what life would be, especially at certain times, without hope, to realize something of its value. The human heart that has no hope is pitiable above all others, unless it be the person whose hope is false. Paul indicated that the Christian is of all men most pitiable if Christ did not truly rise from the dead and thereby assure him of a hope that is steadfast and sure.

Let us take time to define this abstract word, hope. Just what is hope? and in particular, what is Christian hope? First, hope is the content of the Christian's faith concerning the future. In a true sense, faith and hope are like Siamese Twins with one heart: they are inseparable. Faith is the acceptance of what God promises concerning the future; hope is the substance of what is believed. Thus in a broad sense, Christian hope includes everything God promises his children in the future. In a more restricted sense, it applies to all that God promises his children beyond death.

Faith is not believing just anything we might choose to believe. Rather, always it is taking God at his word. The only basis for true faith is God's word. In a similar way, the content of our hope, if reliable, must be derived from what God promises us in his word. Any aspect of what we consider hope that is not based on God's Word is no more than wishful thinking. This is the reason we want to be earnest, honest, and open in building our hope.

Because of the source of our hope, we must exercise faith. The human mind would like very much to have supernatural manifestations on which to base its hope, but Paul argued that we are saved in hope and that the very nature of hope forbids sight (Rom. 8:24). What we see is no longer hope; if we could see it, there would be no place for hope. But when we have God's word for it and believe it, then we hope for what he promises. This means that we shall live and die in our faith-hope relationship with God. Because of this fact, we need to cultivate our hope in every way possible.

In the light of what we have said concerning the relation between faith and hope, it should not be difficult for us to understand how we may cultivate our hope. The increase of true faith will produce a greater hope; the clearer and stronger our faith, the brighter our hope. Thus, in order to brighten our hope, we must develop our faith. Paul explained in the book of Romans that faith is born of hearing the Word of God (10:17). In coming to know what God has said, we have a basis for our faith;at the same time, we have a knowledge of the content of our hope. So if we would cultivate our hope, we can do it through getting to know God's Word better. Surely, the Christian heart is genuinely concerned about the things that make up his hope. That concern should be expressed in prayerful efforts to search out and understand God's revelation concerning what he has prepared for his children beyond this life.

We cannot in this brief discussion set forth fully the content of our Christian hope. We can only say that it contains every aspect of our existence after death. We shall live eternally in the presence of God in heaven. Everything we have pointed out here concerning the Christian's condition and home in heaven is a part of our hope. One of the most glorious qualities of our hope is expressed in the phrase used by Paul in Romans 5:2, "We rejoice in hope of the glory of God." There is no greater description of heaven than "the glory of God." Our Christian hope is that we shall spend eternity in the presence of God's glory, and by his grace and in some way that exceeds our wildest imagination, we shall share in that glory.

Our hope should make a world of difference to us day by day. If our faith and hope are real, they have practical value. We are not visionary nitwits existing in an imaginary world, deluded by our wishful thinking. Our hope is practical; it has teeth in it; it really makes sense. John said that everyone who has this hope in him gives himself to living a pure life (1 John 3:3). The stronger our hope, the more Christlike we become, for we are aware that we have Christ in us now, our hope of glory. We do not become so other-worldly we lose sight of this world and its needs. At the same time, we refuse to become so engrossed in this world that we neglect the things that relate to our hope.

Let us mention some of the particular contributions our hope can make to life now. True hope concerning the future makes us patient in waiting for that hope to materialize (Rom 8:25). The stronger our assurance, the more patient we can be. Paul commended the Thessalonians on the patience of their hope. The true value of this fact is realized only when we recognize the fuller meaning of patience. The word is not limited to simply waiting for something to come to pass without being agitated at having to wait. It is the word for steadfastness, especially against opposition. Thus, our hope helps us to hold on, refusing to become discouraged or to quit. We cannot be defeated because our hope assures us that the final victory belongs to us.

Because of this, we are made bold in life and service. When we are steadfast in hope, we need not fear the enemies that assail and threaten us. Paul spoke of the glory of the Christian hope we have mentioned above (2 Cor 3:7-11). He referred to the glory that accompanied the giving of the Law through Moses and concluded that since the temporary came with such glory, surely that which is eternal will come with far greater glory. In verse 12 he equated this with our hope and said that since we have this great hope, we exercise great boldness in proclaiming the greater revelation of God through Jesus Christ.

To get the full force of what this hope did for Paul, we need to study carefully the remainder of 2 Corinthians 3 and

all of chapter 4. This boldness derived from our Christian
hope characterized the early apostles as they preached the
gospel of Christ, even when forbidden to do so and threa-
tened if they disobeyed (see Acts 4). The same truth was
manifested by Jesus in his life and works. John recorded a
most unusual truth about Jesus' attitude toward rendering
lowly service (John 13:3). He said that since Jesus knew he
had come from God and would return to him, he washed the
apostles' feet. The fact of an assured future led Jesus to be
willing to humble himself and to perform any task pertaining
to human need that came up. In a similar way, we as Christians can commit ourselves to any service that will magnify
God; our hope makes the difference. We can exercise a holy
boldness in the face of any opposition because of our hope.

One of the big problems many Christians wrestle with is
doubt. A realization of the content of our hope is the solution
to all our doubts. The nature of our hope is that it rests entirely upon the veracity of God. Is God trustworthy? Would
he make promises he cannot or will not keep? We would not
think to accuse him of being less than totally worthy of our
fullest confidence and trust. Since his Word is the basis of our
hope, we can rest in our hope without fear or uneasiness.

Paul assured the Christians at Rome that "hope putteth
not to shame" (5:5). He meant that the time would never come
when their hope in Christ would betray them and leave them
embarrassed and deserted. What God has promised he will
perform; this is the quality of our hope, and in this we find
assurance that withstands all attacks.

We may still have unanswered questions, but having
hope, we do not shrink back in fear and trembling. Rather, we
tremble with anticipation when we consider the glory of our
hope. The writer of Hebrews expressed this strongly and
clearly, "Wherein God, being minded to show more abundantly unto the heirs of the promise the immutability of his
counsel, interposed with an oath; that by two immutable
things, in which it is impossible for God to lie, we may have
a strong encouragement, who have fled for refuge to lay hold
of the hope set before us: which we have as an anchor of the

soul, a hope both sure and steadfast, and entering into that which is within the veil; whither as a forerunner Jesus entered for us, having become a high priest forever after the order of Melchizedek" (6:6-20). It was in reference to this assurance of Christian hope the song writer penned the words: "How firm a foundation, ye saints of the Lord, Is laid for your faith in His excellent Word! What more can He say than to you He hath said, To you who for refuge to Jesus have fled?" Thus our hope is indeed a very present help in times of doubt.

Likely few of us will ever reach the degree of a realization of hope that placed Paul in a bind. He told the Philippians that he was torn between the desire to enter into the full realization of his hope and be with Christ and his desire to remain on earth serving Christ. There was no doubt in his mind as to the better of the two, nor as to which he preferred, for he knew that to experience the fulfillment of his hope was far better than anything this life has to offer. However, he was willing to forego the immediate realization of his hope in order that he might be used of God to help others to realize the meaning and value of their hope.

When our hope is understood, we can rise above the circumstances of life in the light of it, even though we may find ourselves undergoing severe experiences. On the night before his crucifixion, Jesus told his apostles that they were to pass through a gruelling experience in which they would be filled with sorrow. However, he went on to assure them that he would see them again, and because of this they would rejoice greatly. Their rejoicing would be produced by a fact that would render it indestructible. That fact was his resurrection from the dead. This is the one thing above all else that proves our hope to be steadfast and sure, and it stands for all time to give the Christian cause for rejoicing. We have already referred to Paul's statement in Romans 5:2, "We rejoice in hope of the glory of God." In that reference the emphasis was on the glory of God as a quality of our hope. Here we would emphasize the idea of *rejoicing*. The word Paul used can be translated *"we glory."* It conveys the idea of exulting in triumph; thus, the rejoicing derived from our hope is not just a mere gladness; it is rather a note of full and eternal victory. We glory in our hope! Our glorying is not in self or self-achievements; it is not in the things of this world. It is in Jesus Christ and in the content of the hope we have through him.

Some of us have already learned from experience, and we could earnestly desire that all Christians would come to know, that as we grow older in the years of this life, our hope becomes dearer to our hearts. Someone might comment that this is natural, for as we grow older, we lose much of our ability to enjoy the things of this world and solace ourselves by playing up our hope. It is true that as we grow older, we do lose some of the shallow sensations that captivate this world. It is not true that this is the reason we rejoice more in our hope. If that were true, then the rejoicing would be natural and automatic to aging people. This is not the case, we regret to say, for many people become more hardened as they grow older because they resent their loss of carnal pleasures. No, that is not the case; the reason a Christian comes to appreciate his hope in a greater way as he grows older is because he comes into a fuller understanding of its meaning. We rejoice in our hope, not because we have nothing else, but rather because there is nothing else to compare with it. Paul stated the attitude of all wise Christians when he wrote to the Philippians, "Yea, verily, and I count all things to be loss for the excellency of the knowledge of Christ Jesus my Lord: for whom I have suffered the loss of all things, and do count them but refuse, that I may gain Christ" (3:8). We have learned there is no real profit in gaining the whole world, if, in doing so, we forfeit our hope.

I earnestly *hope* and pray that this book will be used of God to intensify your hope as a child of God. If you are not his child, I could wish nothing for you more important than that you discover the glory of being his child and turn your heart and life to him in the commitment of faith. If you are his child, cultivate your hope as you deepen your faith in knowing the Word of God and in daily fellowship with him as you follow his will and way for your life.

Begin now with Paul in 2 Corinthians 3:12, "Having therefore such a hope"; then go on with him through the remainder of this chapter and on into chapter 4. If you can join him through 4;15, you will be able to exult with him in verses 16-18: "Wherefore we faint not; for though our outward man is decaying, yet our inward man is renewed day by day. For our light affliction, which is for the moment, worketh for us more and more exceedingly an eternal weight of glory; while we look not at the things which are seen, but at the things which are not seen: for the things that are seen are temporal; but the things that are not seen are eternal."

DATE DUE